DR. STAFFORD NORTH

Handbook

ON
CHURCH DOCTRINES

Revised and updated
with a special section on Islam

Cover art by Paul Nance

ISBN 13: 978-0-89098-3119

Dedication

Dedicated to:

Students at Oklahoma Christian University and the Memorial Road Church of Christ for whom this material was especially prepared and whose service in the Kingdom of God will be worldwide in scope and eternal in duration.

Table of Contents

Section I
A Review of Religious Beliefs
Compared With the Teachings of the Bible

Section II
Islam

Section III
Study Aids

Preface

This *Handbook* is a book about **doctrine**. Unfortunately, some, in recent years, have sought to force a dilemma about doctrine on the religious world by asking such questions as, "Do you preach doctrine or love?" Such a question makes it appear that one must either act kindly with no reference to doctrine or else speak of doctrine and reject love.

The Scriptures do not support such a dichotomy. Jesus said, "If ye love me, ye will keep my commandments" (John 14:15), and Paul urged "speaking the truth in love" (Ephesians 4:15). One who would follow the Scriptures, then, does not choose either doctrine or love, but gives both a place of importance. While this study focuses on **doctrine**, it also seeks to encourage **love** within and without the brotherhood of Christ's body.

Since the *Handbook* is intended more for reference than for persuasion, it may appear rather pointed in its statements about various beliefs. It is the hope of the author, of course, that the treatment of every view represented is both accurate and kind. For the most part, quotations by those who hold a particular doctrine are used as an expression of it.

The scriptures teach that everyone should be ready to give a reason for the hope he has, but with meekness and fear (I Peter 3:15). Such is the spirit in which this work was prepared and, hopefully, the spirit in which it will be received. Each of us should continuously be studying his/her own convictions, for the Scriptures place a strong emphasis on *what one believes*. In the Sermon on the Mount, for example, Jesus warns of false prophets saying, "Not everyone that saith unto me, Lord, Lord, shall enter into the kingdom of heaven" (Matthew 7: 21). In fact, He sent the Holy Spirit to give the apostles *exactly* the message they were to preach (John 16:13; Luke 12:12; John 14:26).

Likewise, when Jesus wrote to the seven churches of Asia (Revelation 1-3), He frequently spoke of the need for a congregation to be true to the doctrines they had received, warning Pergamum and Thyatira to remove false teachers while commending Ephesus and Philadelphia for keeping His Word and rejecting those who were false.

Elders in the church, moreover, are to "be able both to exhort in the sound doctrine, and to convict the gainsayers" (Titus 1:9). And Paul spoke an "anathema" on any who would "preach unto you any gospel other" than what he preached (Galatians 1:8). Paul also urged the disputing Corinthians to "all speak the same thing" (I Corinthians 1:10).

Scores of other New Testament passages testify to the importance of "contend[ing] earnestly for the faith which was once for all delivered unto the saints" (Jude 3) and of the danger of "go[ing] beyond the things which are written" (I Corinthians 4:6).

In the light of such inspired warnings, none of us should say, "Doctrine doesn't matter" or "It doesn't matter what you believe so long as you are sincere"? Surely it matters whether one believes in God and, if it does, whether in the God the Bible describes. And could one expect to be rewarded for such faith if he did not believe and accept God's Son who sacrificed Himself for us? And how could one expect his belief in the Son to be of benefit if he rejected the teachings of the Son or taught others incorrectly of the church which this Son called His bride, His body, His kingdom?

The point is that belief in God and His Son and His spirit involves belief in His message, and there is no promise to one who distorts or confuses it. While God allows us to place our own interpretation on what He has said, we must realize that we will be held responsible for how we have understood and applied His words to our lives (John 12:48; Revelation 20:13).

So let us study carefully the teaching of God's Word. Every one of us should be willing to examine his own beliefs in the light of Scripture in the hope of bringing them as close as possible into harmony with God's will. *Let us never ridicule or treat lightly the beliefs of another; but let us never take lightly what we believe ourselves.*

With an open mind, let us study the beliefs among various churches with the prayer that God will lead us to the fullest possible understanding of His Word, and the strongest possible desire to share our beliefs with others.

Uses For This Book

This *Handbook on Church Doctrines* is designed for two primary uses. First, it may be used as a reference tool to look up what various churches teach on particular points. It collects statements from church sources to indicate the positions they take on various points of doctrine. Second, the book may be used as the basis of a class to study various points of church doctrine, where various churches stand on that point, and how to explain what the Bible teaches on that point. At the back of the book are worksheets for students to use in class as the teacher directs. Also at the back of the book are fourteen lesson plans for teachers to use along with suggestions about how this material can be taught. Lesson 14 is a review. If the teacher has only 13 lesson periods, the review lesson or Lesson 13 on Islam may be skipped. The lesson plans allow for considerable flexibility to fit various age levels and circumstances.

Acknowledgements

Many have been of assistance in the development of these materials, including a host of teachers, preachers, colleagues and writers who have influenced the author over many years. Notable among these are Homer Hailey, under whom the author once took a college class in "Denominational Doctrines," and Roy H. Lanier, Sr., in whose home the author spent many hours during his early life. Special thanks goes to Raymond Kelcy and Morris Thurman for suggestions after reading the manuscript, to Joan Nieman for her tireless efforts in typing and re-typing, and to Lowell Brown for help in the first printing.

The author especially wishes to acknowledge the help of each member of his family: Jo Anne gave valuable suggestions and assisted with research; David, Julie, Linda, and Susan have also helped in many ways.

Appreciation is also extended to Abingdon Press for permission to quote extensively from Frank. S. Meade's *Handbook of Denominations* and to other authors whose works have been used and are listed in the bibliography.

Stafford North
Oklahoma City
September, 1977

Introduction:
A Brief Sketch of Ten Churches

I. Roman Catholic Church

The Catholic church today, as centered in the Vatican in Rome, traces itself back to Jesus and the apostles, and, to some extent, such is true. After the church began on Pentecost and continued for a time, Paul predicted that some would *depart from the faith* (I Timothy 4:1-5; II Timothy 4:3, 4; Acts 20:28-30) and even listed some of the teachings that would characterize this digression: forbidding to marry, commanding to abstain from meats, doctrinal departures.

About the end of the first century, there began a *gradual change* in the doctrine and practice of the church. "The faith which was once for all delivered unto the saints" (Jude 3) was changed in point after point and, while these modifications may have been intended as improvements or clarification, they were, in reality, departures from the "apostles' doctrine" given through inspiration of the Holy Spirit (John 16:13; Galatians 1:7-12). While the changes often were gradual, today one can see clearly the contrast between the Roman Catholic church and the original New Testament church.

A summary of some of these departures will illustrate their nature and extent. The following information is taken largely from *The History of Apostasies* by John F. Rowe, republished in 1956 by John Allen Hudson through The Old Paths Book Club.

1. In the second century there gradually began the tendency for *one of the elders or bishops in a congregation to be regarded as a leader of the others.* This "leading elder" or "the bishop" in a congregation

located in an important city then came to have authority over others in his area. By 325 A.D. this arrangement was given "official" recognition by the Council of Nicea which decreed "that the bishop of each metropolitan church should rule the district attached to that church, and be independent, in his ecclesiastical jurisdiction, of any other bishop" (Rowe, p. 17). At this Council, the Bishops of Rome and Constantinople were given greater *honor* than the others but not greater *authority*.

The Bishop of Rome was first called "Pope" in 400, but he was not then regarded as the "head of the church." Various struggles for power took place with John, Patriarch of Constantinople, first taking the title of "Universal Bishop" in 595. The bishop of Rome at that time was Pelagius II who denounced this move, as did his successor, Gregory, who declared that anyone calling himself the Universal Bishop was a forerunner of the antichrist. In 606, however, the Emperor of Rome took the title away from John of Constantinople and conferred it upon the reigning Bishop of Rome, who, by that time, was Boniface III.

2. About 200, gifts began to be offered to commemorate the martyrs, and this eventually led to *veneration of saints and prayers for the dead.*

3. About 250, a desire to have *more ritual* in the church resulted in the use of *priests*, similar to those of the Old Testament. They were given elaborate vestments, and gradually more and more special ceremonies were practiced. Eventually, many of the heathen customs of special days and great pageantry were incorporated.

4. In the second century, the first discussion on *baptizing infants* took place. After much controversy, it gradually began to be practiced, especially as baptism began to be thought of as the means for erasing *original sin*, a doctrine primarily originated by Augustine in the fourth century.

5. The first person to have water *poured over him rather than be immersed for baptism* appears to have been Novation in 253.

Since he was ill, he had water poured completely over him in his bed. This form of baptism was called "clinical" since it was reserved for those thought to ill to be immersed. For many years these were given a position of second rank, being refused some positions in the church. It was not until around 1200 that sprinkling and pouring for baptism were commonly used.

6. About 350 the remembrance of the Lord's Supper developed into saying "*mass*" through the Latin words, "Ite missa est," a statement which came to be spoken preceding the communion to ask certain ones not allowed to partake to leave. Eventually the word "missa" or "mass" came to be the name of the communion service.

7. About 500, *images* were used in churches as historical memorials. Eventually, however, they began to be used as objects of special use in worship.

8. Music and church historians agree that no *instruments of music* were used in Christian worship during the first century. Gregory the Great spoke against them, and so did Thomas Aquinas in 1250. Occasional use continued, but it was not until about 1400 that the use of organs became very widespread. Even then, they were not used in Eastern churches or in many other places. When the Reformation Movement began, Calvin, Knox, and many others opposed their use.

9. The doctrine of *transubstantiation* (real presence of Christ's body in the bread and His blood in the wine) was first promoted about 700 and was not generally accepted until well after 800.

10. *Marriage of priests* had sometimes been discouraged, but it was not absolutely forbidden until 1074. The resistance was so great that it was 1123 before it was rigidly enforced.

11. In 1483 Pope Sixtus IV issued a "papel bull" authorizing the doctrine of the "*immaculate Conception of Mary*" which decrees that she was born *without* original sin. There was, for many years, great controversy over this matter.

12. In 1564, Pope Pius IV decreed that it is the *role of the church, not individuals, to interpret the Scriptures.*

13. The doctrine of *"papal infallibility"* was decreed in 1870 by the Vatican Council. This teaching says that when the Pope speaks "ex cathedra" or "officially" regarding matters of "faith and morals," he is protected from any error.

The Catholic church retains some of the original doctrines of the church, but its teaching and practice show the result of many departures over the years. It has developed a highly organized hierarchy and very complex system of doctrine.

The drawing below illustrates the gradual departures from apostolic teaching and practice which characterizes the Catholic position.

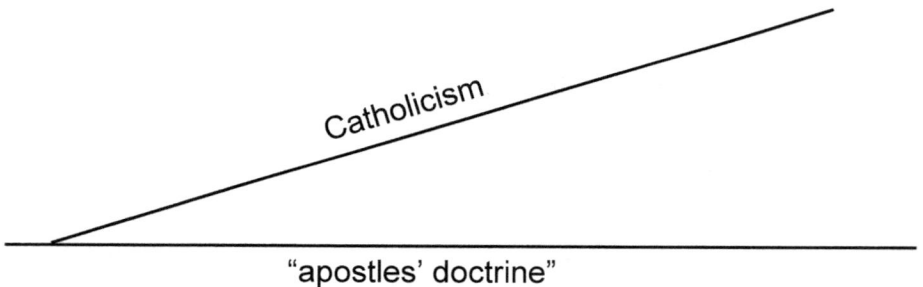

Catholicism

"apostles' doctrine"

Early in the 1500's, *Martin Luther* tried to reform some of the positions of the Roman Catholic Church which he believed were unscriptural. When the Catholic church rejected his proposals and drove him out of the church, he became a prime mover in a new religious movement now called the *Reformation Movement.* Since the Catholic church would not accept reform, those wishing to change had to operate outside the Catholic church. Thus began the *Protestants,* "protesters" against Catholicism.

Luther's position, briefly, was that the Scriptures, and not the Roman Catholic priest or the church, had final authority over conscience. He believed that men could be forgiven of their sins, not by good works or performance of church rites. Especially he opposed the sale of indulgences by the church. Luther believed that salvation was available through man's own Holy Spirit-empowered action in turning from sin directly to God. Mead explains Luther's view this way:

> Justification came through faith and not through ceremony, and faith was not subscription to the dictates of the church but "by the heart's utter trust in Christ." " The just shall live by faith" was the beginning and the end of his thought. He held the individual conscience to be responsible to God alone; he also held that the Bible was the clear, perfect, inspired, and authoritative word of God and guide of man [Mead, *Handbook of Denominations*, pp. 165-166].

This Reformation, however, produced not a united church or even a united Protestantism. Rather, two primary *branches of Protestants* developed: (1) *Evangelical Lutheranism* with Luther and Melanchthon as leaders, and (2) the *Reformed Church* led by John Calvin, Ulrich Zawingli, and John Knox. From these two streams generally have flowed the various Protestant churches.

The drawing below illustrates these branches.

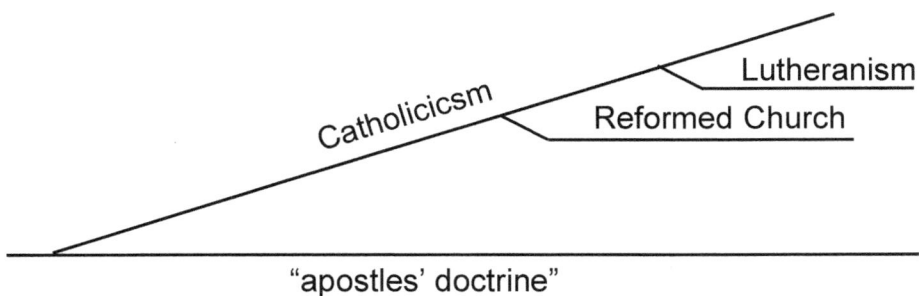

Catholicicsm — Lutheranism / Reformed Church

"apostles' doctrine"

II. Presbyterians

Presbyterianism takes its name from the Greek word "presbuteros" (elder) which describes the system of church government of apostolic times. Basically, Presbyterian beliefs have come from John Calvin and the Reformed church branch of the Protestant Reformation.

Calvin (1509-64), a lawyer, turned to theology and eventually fled France for Geneva, Switzerland, to escape Catholic persecution. Here he quickly became a leader in the Reformed sector of the Reformation.

Calvin's whole thought revolved about the concept of sovereignty: "the sovereignty of God in his universe, the sovereignty of Christ in salvation, the sovereignty of the Scriptures in faith and conduct, the sovereignty of the individual conscience in the interpretation of the Will and Word of God" [Mead, p. 217].

His system has been summarized in five principles: (1) man's inability to do anything to affect his salvation; (2) predestination without conditions; (3) limited atonement; (4) irresistible grace; and (5) perseverance of the saints.

Strictly speaking, Calvin did not begin Presbyterianism, but he did lay the foundations upon which it was reconstructed in Switzerland, Holland, France, England, Scotland, and Ireland. From his work sprang the Huguenots, the Dutch Reformed Church in Holland, and the British Presbyterians who fought against the Catholic Bloody Mary. John Knox made Scotland largely Presbyterian. The Westminster Assembly, a milestone in Presbyterian history, met at the call of Parliament to resolve the struggle over the compulsory use of the Anglican Book of Common Prayer, and it sat for nearly five years (1643-48), in 1,163 sessions, to produce a Larger and Shorter Catechism. These included a directory for the public worship of God, a form of government, and the Westminster Confession of Faith, which became the doctrinal standard of Scottish, British, and American Presbyterianism [Mead, pp. 217-128]. Presbyterians in the United States accepted the Westminster Confession in 1729. This document served as the foundation of Presbyterian belief until 1967 when a revised statement was approved [Mead, p. 222].

III. Baptists

Baptists constitute one of the major Protestant denominations in the United States with the Southern Baptists, largest of a number of

Baptist groups, claiming about 15 million members on their rolls. Baptists often say they have no founder but Christ and that Baptists have been preaching and practicing since the days of John the Baptist. As a church, however, they began in Holland and England [Mead, p. 35]. The name "Baptist" appeared in various forms in Germany and Switzerland: Pedobaptists, who baptized infants and children; Anti-Pedobaptists opposed infant baptism; and Anabaptists, who rebaptized adults once baptized as children. The Anabaptists held to a literal application of the Word of God in social matters, and were pacifists, opposing the holding of public office and payment of taxes and interest. They rejected infant baptism as unscriptural and insisted upon the separation of church and state. Under persecution they spread all over Europe.

In Holland a group of Mennonites, followers of a former Anabaptist leader named Menno Simons, taught such Anabaptist principles as the Scriptures are the only authority for man's faith and practice, that baptism is a believer's privilege, that church and state should be completely and forever separated, and that church discipline should be rigidly enforced. These Mennonites met and appear to have deeply influenced a group of Baptist Separatists who fled to Amsterdam to escape religious persecutions under James I, many living in Mennonite homes. One of their leaders, John Smyth, "was completely captured by the Mennonite argument. He rebaptized himself and his followers in the Anabaptist, or Baptist, faith and with them organized the first English Baptist Church in 1609" [Mead, p 35].

These first churches were "General" Baptist churches, holding to a general atonement for all men. Later there arose "Particular" Baptist churches, believing in predestination or a limited atonement. The first Particular church in Britain dates back to 1638.

In 1631, Roger Williams came to America where he became a great champion of freedom for faith and conscience. Although at first he was a Separatist, he later organized a Particular or Calvinistic Baptist Church at Providence, Rhode Island. As this effort grew, however, it was challenged by the rise of interest in Arminian (anti-Calvinistic) theology by the preaching of George Whitefield, a

Methodist minister from England. In Baptist churches, Calvinism prevailed. In recent years, many Baptists are holding less strongly to some tenets of Calvinistic theology, although its remains show in much of their teaching.

Baptist churches, although they differ in certain points, are generally agreed upon the following principles of faith: the inspiration of the Scriptures as the rule of life; the freedom of each person to approach God for himself; "the granting of salvation through faith by way of grace and contact with the Holy Spirit, two ordinances—the Lord's Supper and baptism of believers by immersion; the independence of the local church; the church as a group of regenerated believers baptized upon confession of faith; infant baptism as unscriptural and not to be practiced; complete separation of church and state; the immortality of the soul" [Mead, p. 38].

IV. Methodists

The Oxford Methodists were a small group of students at Oxford University who gave stated time to prayer and Bible reading. Their leaders were John and Charles Wesley and George Whitefield. Methodically religious, they talked of the necessity of being justified before they could be sanctified and of the need of holiness in human living. They preached to the common people of England—prisoners, the poor, the hopeless [Mead, p. 183-184].

The Wesleys came to Georgia in 1736—Charles as secretary to General Oglethorpe, and John sent by the Society for the Propagation of the Gospel to preach to the Indians. It was generally an unsuccessful two years for John Wesley but, on the ship coming to the colonies, he met a group of Moravians and was deeply impressed by their piety and humble Christian living. Later, after returning to London, he attended a religions meeting where he heard the preacher read Luther's preface to the Epistle to the Romans and felt his heart "strangely warmed" as he learned of Luther's doctrine of "justification by faith." This thought "was the evangelistic spark that energized his life and started the flame of the Wesleyan revival in England. From the pious Moravians via Wesley came the warmhearted emphases upon conversion and holiness which are still the central themes of Methodism" [Mead, p. 184].

The Church of England, of which Whitefield and the Wesleys were then members, did not agree with their work and closed its doors to them. Much of their preaching was then done in open air with emphasis on "repentance, regeneration, turning from sin, and the wrath to come, justification, holiness and sanctification" [Mead, p. 184].

While Wesley did his best to keep the movement within the Church of England, the great numbers recruited from among the unchurched made a separate organization imperative. In 1739 Wesley drew up a set of general rules which are still followed by Methodists. After the Revolutionary War, Methodism was given a separate existence in America and spread rapidly in the new nation.

Methodists preach and teach doctrines of the Trinity, the natural sinfulness of mankind, man's fall, freedom of the will, justification by faith, sanctification and holiness, and future rewards and punishments. Baptism is administered both to infants and adults, usually by sprinkling. Membership is based upon confession of faith or by letter of transfer from other evangelical churches. Wide freedom is allowed in the interpretation and practice of all doctrine.

V. Disciples of Christ

In the late 1700's and early 1800's, a number of leaders in various Protestant denominations such as the Baptists, Methodists, and Presbyterians, each operating independently of the others, decided that the denominational concept of Christianity was not what God had intended. Each of these sought to reform his own denomination but, meeting too much resistance, he left that church in an effort, not to establish another, but to re-establish the church as it was in the beginning.

As these independent efforts grew, each learned of its similarity to others and, eventually, several of them joined forces. Sometimes they were called disciples of Christ, sometimes churches of Christ, sometimes Christian churches. Their principal stand was that the Bible was the complete guide and there should be no man-made creeds. They sought to use the New Testament as a blueprint, doing only what it authorized and leaving off anything it did not authorize. They urged speaking where the Bible speaks, and being silent when the Bible is silent.

For many years this effort grew rapidly but, after the Civil War, a division developed between those who held rigidly to having biblical authority for every practice and those who thought actions not condemned by the Scriptures could be allowed.

Instrumental music in worship and missionary societies were approved by one group as "not condemned" while the other said these should not be allowed because the Scriptures did not specifically authorize them.

During the last quarter of the nineteenth century, this division grew even wider, and by 1906 the rupture was virtually complete. The more conservative group referred to themselves as the church of Christ while the more liberal group called themselves the Christian Church.

In the 1940's and 50's a liberal wing of the Christian church developed which followed the liberal current in many denominations—a less strict interpretation of Scriptures, questioning of biblical miracles, acceptance of members by transfer from denominations without baptism, more emphasis on social progress, and acceptance of the denominational rather than the nondenominational approach. In 1968 a whole new design of church government was accepted at a general meeting of the Christian Church and, with this action, there came a rather sharp distinction between the liberal wing known as the Disciples of Christ and the more conservative wing known still as the Christian Church.

These more conservative churches generally use instrumental music, have elders appointed for terms, and accept missionary societies, but in most respects still are similar in belief to others in the movement to restore New Testament Christianity.

VI. Seventh-day Adventists

The name of this group describes two of their most strongly-held beliefs: (1) that the *Sabbath* or Seventh Day of the Old Testament is still the special day for worship of God; and (2) that the *"advent"* or coming of Christ will bring in a special 1000-year reign on earth.

Seventh-day Adventism of today has sprung from several roots. In the early 1800's there were many who believed that their day would see the return of Christ. A leader among these was *William Miller* who, in 1818, predicted Christ's return in 1843. Later, based on his interpretation of the 70 weeks and the 2,300 days of Daniel 8 and 9, he set the date between March 21, 1843 and March 21, 1844. Some of his associates picked October 23, 1844, as the time.

When these times passed with no return of Christ, Miller stopped predicting and most of his followers disbanded. Some of them, however, formed new groups of their own and by 1860, these had united to form the Seventh-day Adventist Church.

Generally, they believe in the following: (1) that worship should be on the seventh day; (2) that in 1844 Christ moved from the "holy place" of heaven to the "most holy place" of heaven and there began His *"investigative judgment"* to determine the worthiness of believers to enter into eternal life; (3) that the *coming of Christ will be soon* and that when He comes, He will establish His *earthly kingdom for 1,000 years;* (4) that the *dead are in an unconscious state* and that they will be given a new life in the resurrection; (5) that the *gift of prophecy* is still available today; (6) that the *human body* should be well cared for and not abused by alcoholic beverages, tobacco, or the promiscuous use of drugs (Mead, p. 20).

One of the early leaders among the Seventh-day Adventists was *Ellen G. White*, who claimed the gift of prophecy. In one of her many "visions" she said she saw the 10 commandments with the fourth one (Remember the Sabbath) with a halo of light around it. This, she said, emphasized that it was still binding.

VII. Church of Jesus Christ of Latter-Day Saints (Mormons)

Joseph Smith founded the Latter Day Saints in 1830 in Fayette, New York. He claimed to have been visited by God and Jesus Christ in 1820 and by the angel Moroni in 1823. In 1827, this angel told him where to dig up some *golden plates* which told the story, in Reformed Egyptian Hieroglyphics, of the early inhabitants of America. Smith claims to have translated these plates and published this work in 1830 as *The Book of Mormon*. The book gets its title from "Mormon," whose hand is said to have written the original material.

The *Book of Mormon* claims to be the account of what happened in America from 600 B.C. to 421 A.D. It names the Jaredites, one of the groups dispersed from the Tower of Babel, as the original *settlers of America* and says a group of Jews who left Jerusalem in 600 B.C. came to America and became the beginning of the *American Indians.*

Smith also wrote the *Pearl of Great Price* and the *Book of Doctrine and Covenants* to report his many "revelations from God" and to tell how he received the *Book of Mormon.*

These three books are given *equal authority with the Bible* and are said to restore "parts" of the gospel and "many covenants of the Lord" (I Nephi 13:26-28).

During the two years Joseph Smith was "translating" the Book of Mormon, he looked into a hat containing stones called the *Urim and Thummin* which he said came with the plates. He dictated what he saw to Oliver Cowdrey. On May 15, 1829, Smith claims that John the Baptist appeared in person to him and Cowdrey to confer on them the "Aaronic Priesthood" and to tell them to baptize each other, which they did. Smith also claimed that Peter, James, and John visited them and bestowed upon them "the Priesthood of Melchizedek" and the keys of apostleship.

On *April 6, 1830*, Smith, with two brothers, Cowdrey, and two others founded the Church of Jesus Christ of Latter Day Saints. From these six, the word was spread and opposition began almost immediately. In 1830, the Mormons left New York for Kirtland, Ohio. Another group settled at Independence, Missouri. In 1838-39, the group in Missouri was expelled and they settled in Nauvoo, Illinois. Violence erupted there which, in 1844, resulted in the imprisonment and then the *mob murder of Joseph Smith and his brother.*

Brigham Young became the new leader and led the majority of Mormons to Utah where, in 1847, they settled the valley near the Great Salt Lake.

Mormon belief is based on the Bible, "as far as it is translated correctly," the *Book of Mormon,* and the two books which record revelations given to Joseph Smith. They believe in the Father, Son, and Holy Ghost, but state that *the Father and the Son have bodies of flesh and bones* as tangible as man's while *the Holy Ghost is a spirit.* They believe that men will be punished for their own individual sins and not for Adam's transgression. All mankind may be saved through the atonement of Christ if they believe in Christ, repent, and are baptized by immersion for the remission of sins. They also practice the laying on of hands for the gift of the Holy Ghost and the observance of the Lord's Supper each Sunday, speaking and interpretation of tongues, visions, prophecy, and healing. They believe that Christ will return to rule the earth from His capitals in Zion and Jerusalem following the restoration of the 10 tribes of Israel (Mead, p. 99).

The practice of *baptism for the dead* is based upon I Corinthians 15:29 and allows the opportunity for someone living to be baptized for one who has already died (Mead, p. 99). "Marriage for eternity" suggests that there is a difference between being married for this life and for the next life. Under this teaching, one may have one wife for time and a different one for eternity. Also, a comment should be made that Joseph Smith taught that *plural marriage* was acceptable and it was practiced by many Mormons, including both Smith and Young. The U.S. government required that the practice be stopped and the church "re-interpreted" its teaching and now it is not taught or practiced with the approval of church leaders.

There are *two major branches* of the Latter Day Saints. The larger one is headquartered in Salt Lake City. The smaller one, called Reorganized, rejects the leadership of Brigham Young, and is based in Independence, Missouri (see Mead, pp. 102-103).

VIII. Jehovah's Witnesses

Charles T. Russell is the organizer of the Jehovah's Witnesses, a name adopted in 1931. It was earlier, in 1879, however, that Russell founded "Zion's Watch Tower," known today as "The Watch Tower Announcing Jehovah's Kingdom." Russell taught and wrote widely and collected many followers. Many charges were laid against him personally, including court cases involving divorce, "Miracle Wheat," which he sold at high prices, and libel suits he brought against others. The court cases show that he was not honest in his dealings and often presented false information.

After Russell died in 1916, *Judge Joseph Franklin Rutherford* took leadership of the group and, like Russell, wrote voluminously. *Nathan H. Knorr* became the president after Rutherford's death in 1942.

The focus of the Jehovah's Witnesses is on Christ's return which they have been predicting was close at hand for many years. Russell first predicted, for example, that the consummation of the "time of the end" would see "the full establishment of the kingdom of God in the earth at A.D. 1914" (Russell, *Thy Kingdom Come*, p. 126). Rutherford, in his *Millions Now Living Will Never Die,* predicted on page 97 that since "1925 shall mark the resurrection of the faithful worthies of old and the beginning of reconstruction, it is reasonable to conclude that millions of people now on earth will still be on the earth in 1925. Then, based upon the promises set forth in the Divine Word, we must reach the positive and indisputable conclusion that millions now living will never die."

Another major prediction of the Jehovah's Witnesses was that "Six thousand years from man's creation will end in 1975, and the seventh period of a thousand years of human history will begin in the fall of 1975 C.E.... It would not be by mere chance or accident...for the reign of Jesus Christ...to run parallel with the seventh millennium of man's existence" (*Life Everlasting in Freedom of the Sons of God*, pp. 29-30). Although this prediction was put in cautious language, it indicates they expected the millennium to start in 1975.

Jehovah's Witnesses meet in "Kingdom Halls" and have an extensive missionary program. They do not make a distinction between "clergy" and "laity" and do not use terms like "reverend." Most members devote 15 hours a month in "preaching"; pioneers are required to work 100 hours a month; special pioneers must work 150 hours a month. All workers, including those at headquarters in Brooklyn, serve voluntarily and at their own expense except for a few who receive small expense allowances.

The view of the Jehovah's Witnesses is that Satan ruled the world until 1914. At that time Jesus began to rule. In 1918 He came into the Temple of Jehovah and began sending His followers out to preach.

God is now gathering His people who will be given life in the new world. The Battle of Armageddon will come soon to destroy false churches, human governments, and commercial businesses, all of which are regarded as allies of Satan. This is why they will not salute a national flag, bear arms, or participate in government.

After Armageddon, a new world can be started by Jesus and His followers. The righteous dead will be raised to take part but the wicked dead are never raised. One special group, a literal 144,000, will reign with Christ in heaven while other believers will live in earthly paradise.

IX. Assemblies of God

In 1914 several *Pentecostal churches and assemblies* combined their efforts into the General Council of the Assemblies of God. The million members of the Assemblies of God accept the Bible as inspired and are generally regarded as fundamentalists. They believe in baptism of the Holy Spirit, evidenced by tongue-speaking; promote holy living; accept divine healing; and look for the second coming of Christ to be followed by a 1,000-year reign on earth. They believe all gifts of the Spirit are active today. They practice water baptism and the Lord's Supper and believe in "entire sanctification." Local churches are independent in the conduct of their affairs but there is a district organization and a general council in which each congregation has one delegate and in which all ordained ministers participate.

X. Church of the Nazarene

The Church of the Nazarene is the result of the merger of several independent groups which sprang up in the late 19th century. Each group was started to promote *personal holiness* much like the Wesleys did a century earlier. The most important of these mergers took place in 1907 and 1908. They do not practice speaking in tongues but do believe in divine healing today.

Nazarenes admit members on the basis of a confession of faith and an agreement to observe the rules of the church. They practice baptism by sprinkling, pouring, or immersion, and believe that "sanctification" is a special experience that comes after one has been regenerated.

The church has a general assembly, district assemblies and local congregations.

Section I

A Review of Religious Beliefs Compared With the Teachings of the Bible

I. The Nature of God

A. The Trinity, including views of the Son and Holy Spirit

All the churches being considered here have generally a biblical view except two: Latter Day Saints and Jehovah's Witnesses.

1. **Latter Day Saints (Mormons)**

   a. *God has a material body:*

   "The Father has a body of flesh and bone as tangible as man's; the Son also, but the Holy Ghost has not a body of flesh and bones but is a personage of Spirit..." (*Doctrine and Covenants*, Sec. 130:22).

   "We affirm that to deny the materiality of God's person is to deny God; for a thing without parts has no whole and an immaterial body cannot exist" (Talmage, *Articles of Faith*, pp. 48, 466-467).

   (See John 4:24 and Luke 24:39; Colossians 1:15.)

   b. *God was once a man and became God; we can become gods in the same way:*

   "Mormon prophets have continuously taught the sublime truth that God the eternal father was once a mortal man who passed through the school of earth—life similar to that through which we are now passing. He became God—an exalted being, through obedience to the same eternal gospel truth that we are given opportunity today to obey" (Hunter, *The Gospel Through the Ages*, pp. 105).

   (See Genesis 1:1—God was "in the beginning.")

"When our father Adam came into the Garden of Eden, he came into it with a celestial body and brought Eve, one of his celestial wives, with him....He is our father and our God and the only God with whom we have to do" (Brigham Young, *The Journal of Discourses*, Vol. I, p. 50).

(See Matthew 22:30; Genesis chapters 1-3.)

c. *There are many gods*—obviously if all can become gods, there can be many:

Orson Pratt said, "In the heaven where our spirits were born, there are many gods, each of whom has his own wife or wives which were given to him previous to his redemption while yet in his mortal state" (Pratt, *The Seer*, Vol. I, p. 37; quoted in Martin, *Kingdom of the Cults*, p. 182).

(See Isaiah 43:10; 44:6.)

d. *Christ was not begotten by the Holy Spirit but by the father in heaven:*

"When the virgin Mary conceived the child Jesus, the father had begotten him in his own likeness. He was not begotten by the Holy Ghost. And who was the father? He was the first of the human family...Jesus our elder brother was begotten in the flesh by the same character that was in the Garden of Eden and who is our father in heaven" (Brigham Young, *Journal of Discourses*, Vol. I, pp. 50-51).

(See Matthew 1:18-20.)

e. *Confusion between "Father" and "Son."*

"Behold I am he who has prepared from the foundation of the world to redeem my people. Behold, I am Jesus Christ. I am the Father and the Son" (*Book of Mormon*, Ether 3:14).

(See John 16:28.)

2. **Jehovah's Witnesses**

a. *Jehovah is the one God and there is no Trinity.*

"There was, therefore, a time when Jehovah was all alone in universal space. All life and energy and thought were contained in him alone....Then the time came when Jehovah began to create" (*Let God Be True*, p. 25).

b. Christ was created and was not eternal.

"During all this creative activity, Jehovah had beside him a helper—a 'master worker'—the most beloved of all his angelic sons in the invisible heavens" Proverbs 8:30 (*Good News to Make You Happy*, p. 69).

"As He (Christ) is the highest of Jehovah's creation, so also He was the first, the direct creation of God, the only begotten" Rev. 21:13 (Russell, *Studies in the Scriptures*, Vol. V, p. 84).

"Jesus was not half God, half man. He was not God in the flesh. To atone for 'one man's (Adam's) trespass,' 'the one man Jesus Christ' had to correspond exactly to the once perfect Adam. He had to be a perfect man, nothing more, nothing less." Romans 5:15 (*Good News*, p. 118).

"This Son is described as 'only begotten' because He is the first and only direct creation of God" (*Good News*, p. 117).

"Who ran the universe during the three days that Jesus was dead and in the grave….If Jesus was God, then during Jesus' death God was dead and in the grave….If Jesus was the immortal God, he could not have died" (*Let God Be True*, p. 109).

Teaching of the Scripture on God, Christ and the Holy Spirit

1. John 1:3 says that *nothing* was created except what the Word created, so the Word is the creator of all, not a created being.
2. John 1:1 says *the Word existed "in the beginning"* and thus existed before creation began.
3. Jehovah's Witnesses translate John 1:1 "the Word was a god" but Isaiah 43:10 and 45:21 declare that *there is no God beside Jehovah.* So either the Word is included in Jehovah or else he is a false God.
4. Isaiah 7:14 and Matthew 1:23 says that *Jesus was "God with us."*
5. In John 5:17-18, Jesus calls God His Father which, the Bible declares, was *making Himself equal with God.* This the Jews also understood for they tried to stone Him for blasphemy—or making Himself God.

6. John 8:58 is a similar passage where the Jews also seek to stone Him because He applies the phrase *"I Am"* to Himself when this can only be applied to God (Exodus 3:14). See also John 10:30.

7. Philippians 2:5-8 states that Jesus *had been equal with God* but gave that up to take the form of a man.

8. In Colossians 1:15-17 Jesus is declared to be the *image of the invisible God;* the firstborn (first in rank like a firstborn son) of all creation; the creator of all; eternal, since He was before all. The Jehovah's Witness translation inserts the word "other" in several places in these verses with absolutely no warrant from the Greek.

9. Colossians 1:15 says Christ is the *image* of the invisible God; Colossians 2:9 says *all the fullness of the Godhead* dwelt in Him when He was in the flesh; and Hebrews 1:2-3 says He is *the very image of God's substance.* These passages show that Christ possessed all the same attributes of God and is, therefore, part of the Trinity.

10. Christ is called God in Isaiah 9:6, Titus 2:13, I John 5:20, and many other Scriptures.

11. Thomas called Christ *"My Lord and my God."* In the Greek, this is *"the* Lord of me and *the* God of me" (John 20:28).

12. Jesus said that He was to be honored *"even as they honor the Father"* (John 5:23).

13. *God* is called "the first" and "the last" in Isaiah 44:6 but the same is applied to *Christ* in Revelation 1:17-18.

14. God will not give His glory to another, but *did give His glory to Christ*—Isaiah 48:11 and John 17:15.

15. Jesus said, "I am in the Father, and the Father in me," (John 14:10) thus declaring that they are *both of the same essence.*

16. *The Godhead is composed of three equal, unified, but separate personalities*—Acts 17:29; Colossians 2:9; Matthew 3:16, 17; 28:8; Jude 20, 21; I John 4:12-15; I Peter 1:2; II Corinthians 13:14; Romans 8:9, 10.

17. Because God is called "one" (Deuteronomy 6:4) does not mean there cannot be a Trinity. The Hebrew word translated "one" is *echod,* which can mean a *composite unity* as in Genesis 2:24 where two people are called "one" or in Numbers 13:23 where many grapes are called "one" bunch.

18. *Regarding the Trinity, there are several possibilities:*
    a. That there is one God with the Holy Spirit and the Word being subordinate deities.
    b. That there are three separate and distinct beings, each a separate God in His own right.
    c. That there is only one God but He appears in different forms.
    d. That there is one God composed of three equal but distinct personalities which can be viewed as having the same attributes and the same purpose, but sometimes functioning separately. When one rejects the position of the Jehovah's Witnesses (a) they seek to force on him either (b) or (c). The Scriptures, however, teach that (d) is correct.

B. Supernatural and Miracles Today

1. Catholic Church

Catholics accept biblical miracles and believe in miracles such as healings today. For one to be named a saint, for example, he must have performed a specified number of "certified" miraculous deeds. Catholics generally do not practice Holy Spirit baptism but do allow those who feel they have certain gifts such as tongues to practice this belief. With the "sacrament of confirmation," the priest lays hands on the person to bestow on them the Holy Spirit but this does not imply that all receive the gifts of the Holy Spirit (see Gibbon, *Faith of our Father*, pp. 230-33. Also see Edward O'Connor, *Perspectives on Charismatic Renewal*, in which this Catholic professor outlines the Catholic teaching and practice).

2. Baptist Church

Some accept the idea of charismatic gifts and some do not.

3. Methodist Church

Some accept the idea of charismatic gifts and some do not. Oral Roberts, for example, joined the Methodist church.

4. Presbyterian Church

Some accept the idea of charismatic gifts and some do not.

5. Disciples of Christ

Some accept the idea of charismatic gifts and some do not.

6. Latter Day Saints

Joseph Smith obviously believed in the appearance of angels and modern-day revelation. Both he and Brigham Young, as well as others, are considered prophets. Smith claimed to speak in tongues as do others in Mormonism. Smith made many predictions under the claim of inspiration. Article 7 of the Articles of Faith says, "we believe in the gift of tongues, prophecy, revelation, visions, healing, interpretations of tongues, etc."

7. Jehovah's Witnesses

"When the apostles passed off the earthly stage, the imparting of miraculous gifts passed away with them." When the church had become firmly established, "the miraculous gifts of its infancy would be needed no more and would be put away." "Miraculous gifts of the Spirit are not bestowed upon the remnant today of members of Christ's body" (*This Means Everlasting Life*, p. 169).

8. Seventh-day Adventists

Seventh-day Adventists believe in gifts of the Spirit today and, in particular, that Ellen G. White possessed the gift of prophecy. "Ellen G. White is 'recognized' as one who possessed the gift of the spirit of prophecy" (*Seventh-day Adventists Answer Questions on Doctrine*, p. 91).

"We know that some earnest Christians have the impression that gifts ceased with the apostolic church. But Adventists believe that the closing of the Scripture canon did not terminate Heaven's communication with men through the gifts of the Spirit, but rather that Christ by the ministry of His spirit guides His people, edifying and strengthening them, and especially so in these last challenging days of human history" (*Questions on Doctrine*, pp. 93-95).

9. Assemblies of God

"Believers of all ages are promised that they may be filled with the Holy Spirit as the disciples were in the apostolic age (Acts 2:38, 39)." One may know when he has been filled with the Spirit because "he will speak in other tongues as the Spirit gives him utterance. (cf. Acts 2:4; 10:45, 46; 19:6; I Corinthians 14:18.)" All other gifts of the Spirit also are available today (Ralph M. Riggs, *We Believe*, pp. 113-114).

10. Church of the Nazarene

Nazarenes believe in baptism of the Holy Spirit today and in "divine healing." Sanctification comes after regeneration and with the baptism of the Holy Spirit.

"We believe in the Bible doctrine of divine healing and urge our people to seek to offer the prayer of faith for the healing of the sick. Providential means and agencies when deemed necessary should not be refused" (*Manual, Church of the Nazarene*, 1968, p. 34).

The Teaching of the Scripture on Miracles

1. The term "miracle" means a "sign" or act of God which is above and beyond what we understand the laws of nature to allow, such as an immediate and complete healing, a raising from the dead, striking someone blind, walking on water, drinking deadly poison with *no* ill effects. God still acts, answers prayers, heals, and sustains but does not do these things as "sign," and His healings now are "within" rather than "beyond" natural laws. These beneficial acts are accepted by faith and are regarded as "providential" rather than "miraculous" since they are not "signs." In healing today, God uses doctors and medicines and healing takes time. This is distinct from the immediate and complete healings of the Bible.

2. The *purpose of miracles* was to confirm a message as a revelation from God (Mark 16:15-20; John 3:1, 2; I Corinthians 14:22; Hebrews 2:3, 4). It was never intended that healings and other miracles would be for the universal benefit of man.

3. The power to work miracles was made available to Christians only through *the laying on of the apostles' hands* (Acts 8:5-18; 19:1-6; II Timothy 1:6; Romans 1:11). The *only two exceptions* to this were the *apostles* on Pentecost (once on Jews) and the *household of Cornelius* (once on Gentiles) in which the Holy Spirit came directly from God and is, therefore, called "baptism of the Holy Spirit" (Acts 1:5; 10:44-46; 11:15-18). These passages show that these were special events unlike any other for when Peter explained the happenings at Cornelius' house, he skipped over ten years of history to say what came to Cornelius was like what came "even as on us at the beginning" (Acts 11:15). Such a statement implies that these two stand apart from all others and, indeed, these are the only two accounts anywhere in the New Testament church of the Holy Spirit bringing miraculous power except by laying on of the apostles' hands.

4. I Corinthians 12, 13, and 14 are devoted to the gifts of the Spirit. In chapter 13:8-13, Paul points to the superiority of love over spiritual gifts because love is lasting while *gifts are temporary*, being needed only in the childhood or immature stage of the church. Gifts of prophecy, tongues, and supernatural knowledge, for example, are to cease when the "parts" they supplied made up the "perfect" or complete revelation. When the revelation was fully given, the means of revelation would no longer be needed nor would confirming signs such as healings.

5. A *close examination of so-called "miracles" of today* reveal a wide difference between them and those of the Bible. *Then*, they were instantaneous, complete healings of an observable malady while today they are neither instantaneous, complete, or observable. *Then*, persons well known and certified dead were raised. *Now*, any dead beings raised are in some far away, unverifiable event. *Then*, tongue-speaking was an utterance in a known and recognizable

foreign language "unknown" only in the sense that the speaker had not learned it, while *now* it is an ecstatic utterance usually in an emotional state.

6.   As may be noted by the list of churches that either support or allow miracles today, *those who claim gifts of the Spirit cover a very wide range of religious belief.* Miracles are claimed by the Mormons to prove the *Book of Mormon,* by the Catholics to determine saints, by Seventh-day Adventists to prove the Sabbath as still binding, by those who accept predestination as a demonstration that one is of the elect, by Nazarenes to give sanctification. Each person who considers himself to have received a gift of the Spirit is sure that his is genuine. Those who claim such an experience consider theirs to be true but will usually admit that some others with the same claim may be in error. Obviously, *all who claim miraculous gifts cannot be right.* Not only do they preach different doctrines, but their doctrines are contradictory. If miracles are to confirm the word, whose word is being confirmed? They cannot all be right; they could all be wrong.

II. The Nature of Man

A. The nature of the soul

Of the groups being studied, two hold to the view that a man does not have an eternal soul. Both the Jehovah's Witnesses and the Seventh-day Adventists (also the World Wide Church of God) take this position.

1. Jehovah's Witnesses

"The Hebrew word, *nephesh*, which occurs about 750 times in the Bible, means actually a 'breather'. As we have already seen, fish, birds, animals, and humans are all called 'souls (nephesh)' in the Bible. They do not *have* souls. They *are* souls, breathing creatures, and as the Psalms quoted above show, the 'soul' cannot escape the hand of gravedom. It dies. Examination of the 102 occurrences in the Greek Scriptures of the corresponding word *psyche* likewise shows that man is a soul" (*Good News*, p. 88). Scripture references cited are Psalms 89:48; 6:4-5; I Corinthians 15:45; Genesis 3:19; Matthew 10:28; Ezekiel 18:4; Acts 3:23; Ecclesiastes 3:19-20; 9:5, 10; 12:7. (Also see *Let God Be True*, pp. 66-75.)

2. Seventh-day Adventists

"We as Adventists believe that, in general, the Scriptures teach that the soul of man represents the whole man, and not a particular part independent of the other component parts of man's nature; and further, that the soul of man cannot exist apart from the body, for man is a unit....We, as Adventists, have reached a definite conclusion that man rests in the tomb until the resurrection morning. Then, at the first resurrection (Rev. 20:4, 5), the resurrection of the just (Acts 24:15), the righteous come forth immortalized at the call of Christ, the Lifegiver, and *they can enter into life everlasting* in their eternal home in the kingdom of glory" (*Questions on Doctrine*, pp. 515, 520).

3. Garner Ted Armstrong, of the Worldwide Church of God

In a commentary on Genesis 2:7, Armstrong says, "Man *became* a living soul; that is what man is—a *soul*. Notice there is no mention that man has a soul, but that man *is* a soul" (*Do You Have an Immortal Soul?*, p. 10). "Death is the absence of life, the cessation of life—not the continuation of life under different circumstances. Notice the two opposite states given in Romans 6:23. God tells us the wages of sin is death, but, on the other hand, the gift of God (not something you were born with) is eternal life through Jesus Christ" (*Do You Have an Immortal Soul?*, p. 11).

The Teaching of the Scripture on the Soul

1. The question is not whether the words "spirit" and "soul" are sometimes used to refer to the life principle which inhabits both man and animal and which ceases at death (Genesis 2:7; Revelation 16:3). The words do sometimes have this meaning. But often a word has more than one meaning such as "heaven" which may refer to the air where birds fly or to the dwelling place of God. The question, rather, is, "Do *some passages* use 'soul' or 'spirit' in a way which indicates a part of man which continues to live after death?" If so, the fact that there are passages which use the word "soul" or "spirit" in a different way will not change the force of these passages.

2. Luke 23:46 says that *Jesus entrusted His spirit to God* at the time of His death. What did He give back to God? Not just His breath but

the soul which continued to live. See also Matthew 27:50 and Acts 7:59.

3. Ecclesiastes 12:7 says *the spirit returns to God* while the body returns to dust.

4. In Philippians 1:21-23, Paul says that *after death he expected to go to Christ.* See also II Corinthians 5:8 and II Timothy 4:6.

5. Mark 12:27 says that *God is not the God of the dead but of the living.* God's people who have departed this life are not dead but alive; for, although their bodies are dead, something is still alive. Examples of this are Moses and Elijah at the transfiguration (Matthew 17:3) and the present tense used about Abraham, Isaac, and Jacob (Luke 20:37, 38).

6. In the story (not called a parable) of the Rich Man and Lazarus (Luke 16:19-31) we have a glimpse of dead persons being *alive while the world continued.* Had such not been the case, Jesus would not have used even a hypothetical story in such a misleading way.

7. A soul is spoken of as *departing at death* or of *existing after death* in the following passages: Genesis 35:18; Luke 8:55; Revelation 6:9; Zechariah 12:1; I Samuel 28:18-19.

8. Man's *spirit or soul acts* in ways that merely "life" cannot: willing, Matthew 26:41; worshipping, John 4:23; receives a witness, Romans 8:16; knowing, I Corinthians 2:11.

9. Man's *spirit* can be *lost* or *saved* (I Corinthians 5:5) and *purified* (I Peter 1:22).

10. Genesis 1:28 says that man is created *in God's image*, but God is spirit (John 4:24). Our bodies are not in His image. There must, then, be something about man which is in the image of the spirit-God, and that is the spirit or soul of man.

B. The Fall and Original Sin

1. Roman Catholic

"Man was created in a state of innocence and holiness...but in consequences of his disobedience [Adam's sin] he fell from his high estate of righteousness; his soul was defiled by sin; he became subject to death and to various ills of body and soul and forfeited his heavenly inheritance.

"Adam's transgression was not confined to himself but was transmitted, with its long train of dire consequences, to all his posterity. It is called *original* sin because it is derived from our original progenitor. (Romans 5:12; Ephesians 2:3; Job 14:4; Psalms 51:5).

"These passages clearly show that we have all inherited the transgression of our first parents and that we are born enemies of God. And it is equally plain that these texts apply to every member of the human family—to the infant of a day old as well as to the adult.

"Now He tells us in His Gospel that Baptism is the essential means established for washing away the stain of original sin and the door by which we find admittance into his church....The church teaches that baptism is necessary for all, for infants as well as adults...." (Gibbons, pp. 219, 220).

2. Baptists

From the New Hampshire Confession of Faith, which Baptists still publish as a statement of their faith, the following statement is found: "We believe that man was created in holiness, under the law of his Maker; but by voluntary transgression fell from that holy and happy state, in consequence of which all mankind are now sinners, not by constraint, but by choice; being by nature utterly void of that holiness required by the Law of God, positively inclined to evil; and therefore under just condemnation to eternal ruin, without defense or excuse." (Romans 5:12, 19; Psalm 51:5; Ezekiel 18:19, 20).

Baptists do not now take this statement to mean that babies are born sinners, but rather that they have an "imperfection" which gives them a "positive inclination to sin." Each one becomes guilty, however, as he chooses sin for himself (Wallace, *What Baptists Believe*, pp. 20-24). Often this state of the infant is called "total hereditary depravity" which suggests, not that we are born already guilty but, rather, that we are born so inclined to sin that it is inevitable. The only way out of this situation is the changed nature that comes when one is "reborn."

3. Methodists

"Original sin standeth not in the following of Adam (as the Pelagians do vainly talk), but it is the corruption of the nature of every man, that naturally is engendered of the offspring of Adam, whereby man is very far gone from original righteousness, and of his own nature inclined to evil, and that continually" (*Methodist Discipline*, pgf. 67). "Sanctification is that renewal of our fallen nature by the Holy Ghost, received through faith in Jesus Christ, whose blood of atonement cleanseth from all sin; whereby we are not only delivered from the guilt of sin; but are washed from its pollution, saved from its power, and are enabled, through faith, to love God with all our hearts and to walk in His Holy commandments blameless" (*Methodist Discipline*, pgf. 86).

Methodists, then, believe in original sin to the extent that man's nature has been corrupted but not that actual guilt is imputed.

4. Presbyterians

"There is something radically wrong with human nature. Man, left to the freedom of choice, sinned, and his sin resulted in corruption of his nature that affected his whole being. Man is prone to evil" (Miller, *Why I am a Presbyterian*, p. 60).

Many Presbyterians, like the Baptists, have modified their view from strict Calvinism. A note in *Barnes Commentary*, for example, at Ephesians 2:3, and at Romans 5:12, gives the "orthodox view" that every man has "imputed guilt" because he is a descendant of Adam and that this is his nature as a "child of wrath."

5. Disciples of Christ

Generally, a scriptural view that man is guilty only from his own sins (Adams, *Why I Am a Disciple of Christ*, p. 53).

6. Latter Day Saints

The second of the thirteen "Articles of Faith of the Church of Jesus Christ of Latter Day Saints" states: "We believe that men will be punished for their own sins, and not for Adam's transgression."

The *Book of Mormon*, however, says in 2 Nephi 2:21b-25, "For he gave commandment that all men must repent; for he showed unto all men that they were lost, because of the transgression of their parents. And now, behold, if Adam had not transgressed, he would not have fallen, but he would have remained in the garden of Eden. And all things which were created must have remained in the same state in which they were after they were created; and they must have remained forever, and had no end. And they would have had no children; wherefore they would have remained in a state of innocence, having no joy, for they knew no misery; all things having been done in the wisdom of him who knoweth all things. Adam fell that men might be; and men are, that they might have joy."

Mormon leader James E. Talmage explains: "Adam found himself in a position that impelled him to disobey one of the requirements of God. He and his wife had been commanded to multiply and replenish the earth. Adam was still immortal; Eve had come under the penalty of mortality; and in such dissimilar conditions, the two could not remain together, and therefore, Adam would be disobeying another command by yielding to his wife's request. He deliberately and wisely decided to stand by the first and greater commandment; and, therefore, with a full comprehension of the nature of his act, he also partook of the fruit that grew on the tree of knowledge. The fact that Adam acted understandingly in this matter is affirmed by the scriptures..." (Talmage, *Articles of Faith*, p. 68).

"The Mormon Catechism puts the whole matter more briefly and bluntly: 'Was it necessary that Adam should partake of the forbidden fruit? Answer: Yes, unless he had done so he would not have known good and evil here, neither could he have moral posterity....Did Adam and Eve lament or rejoice because they had transgressed the commandment? Answer: They rejoiced and praised God"" (Gerstner, *The Theology of the Major Sects*, p. 46).

7. Jehovah's Witnesses

"All of Adam's offspring were born after his disobedience. Thus, his offspring inherited sin and death from him. All men inherit imperfection, because all come from Adam and Eve. As the Bible book of Job tells us: 'Who can produce someone clean out of someone unclean? There is not one' (Job 14:4). Also, at Romans 5:12 the Bible explains: 'Through one man [Adam] sin entered into the world and death through sin, and thus death spread to all men.' Just as a perfect piece of machinery cannot be produced from an imperfect mold, so Adam in his imperfection could not produce perfect children, free from sin.—(Psalm 51:5)" (*The Truth that Leads to Eternal Life*, p. 32).

"However, it is one thing to make unintentional mistakes because of inherited sin, but entirely another matter deliberately to practice what one knows to be wrong. (I John 5:16) If one is truly repentant over mistakes he makes because of inherited weaknesses, he can expect merciful forgiveness from God (Proverbs 28:13). But he must be careful that, once he knows what is right, he does not deliberately choose to follow a course contrary to God's will. To do so would mean loss of God's favor and of life itself.—Deuteronomy 30:15-20; Hebrews 10:26, 27" (*The Truth*, p. 33).

8. Seventh-day Adventists

Man was born sinless but when Adam sinned, he brought sin to everyone. "Sin...is an inheritance. Men are born sinners" (Branson, *Drama of the Ages*, p. 43).

9. Assemblies of God

After Adam and Eve sinned, "their understanding became darkened, their hearts became wicked, and their bodies became subject to disease and death" (Ephesians 4:18).

"Through Adam, sin entered into the world and death by sin; and since all have sinned, all suffer the results of sin" (Romans 5:12). Sinners "shall be punished wil everlasting destruction from the presence of the Lord" (Ezekiel 18:4; Revelation 21:8).

Christ did not inherit "a sinful human nature from his mother"; rather, a "special body was prepared Him in which was no sin" (Hebrews 10:5) (Riggs, *We Believe*, pp. 95-96).

10. Church of the Nazarene

"We believe that original sin, or depravity, is that corruption of the nature of all offspring of Adam by reason of which everyone is very far gone from original righteousness or the pure state of our first parents at the time of their creation, is averse to God, is without spiritual life, and inclined to evil, and that continually. We further believe that original sin continues to exist with the new life of the regenerate, until eradicated by the baptism with the Holy Spirit" (*Manual*, p. 29).

The Teaching of the Scripture on Original Sin

1. Romans 5:12 does teach that Adam brought physical death on all and so we all suffer some *consequences* of his sin, but it does not teach that we are *guilty* because of his sin.
2. Ezekiel 18:20 says, "the son shall not bear the iniquity of the father," rather "the soul that sinneth, it shall die."
3. Romans 3:23 states that *all have sinned* and it is for our own sins that we are responsible to God.
4. I John 3:4 states that "everyone that doeth sin doeth also lawlessness; and sin is lawlessness." James 4:17 says that "to him therefore that knoweth to do good, and doeth it not, to him it is sin." These passages show that it is not the sin of another but, rather, *for our own transgression or omission that we are guilty.*
5. Matthew 18:3—we are to become like *little children* to enter the kingdom.

6. Psalm 51:5 says "in sin did my mother conceive me." *This verse does not state that David was born a sinner.* If it refers to an actual sin which someone did, then his mother did it, not he. Taken in its context, however, we see that David is speaking of his own sin with Bathsheba, and his reference to being "conceived in sin" is a hyperbole to suggest the great sense of guilt which he felt for this sin he committed long after his birth. The entire psalm is filled with such figurative expression.

7. Ephesians 2:3 says that we are "by nature children of wrath." This passage, along with many others, indicates that *man has a tendency to sin* because he often seeks fulfillment of natural desires in ways that God has restricted. This does not, however, suggest that he is born to sin. There is no Scripture which says that man's tendency to sin was changed by Adam's sin. Obviously, Adam and Eve, even before their sin, were subject to the same temptations we are—lust of flesh, lust of eyes, pride of life. While the more sin that surrounds us the more difficult it may be to resist the temptation to sin, man was created with the possibility of lust and sin. Adam and Eve succumbed, and so has each of us.

8. The Catholics are consistent in saying that if infants are born to sin, then there must be some immediate provision for their salvation—infant baptism. That such is not God's plan, however, is evident from the complete absence of any such teaching in the Bible. To be sure that an infant which may die in the mother's womb can receive baptism before he dies, Catholics even baptize such a child before birth. Such is totally out of harmony with the design and purpose of New Testament baptism. To be consistent, however, others who hold to original sin should make a similar effort to get forgiveness for infants.

C. Predestination

1. Catholic Church

The Catholic Church believes that *salvation is available to anyone* and rejects the Calvinistic idea of some being predestined to salvation and others to damnation.

2. Baptists

The Baptist church is *divided* on the question of predestination. Early in their history, the Calvinist view of predestination was quite strong. "Primitive Baptists," for example, still hold to this view. "Free-Will Baptists" reject the Calvinistic view of predestination. "Missionary Baptists" have moved away from the Calvinistic position as suggested by one of their own number, William W. Adams: "Let it be remembered that, less than a hundred years ago, all five points of Calvin's system of theology generally prevailed among Baptists, as theological textbooks of the times will confirm. Today, only one point remains to any appreciable extent among Baptists, inevitable perseverance [once saved, always saved] and there is growing evidence that Baptists are increasingly questioning this last vestige of the central core of Calvin's system of theology" (from introduction to Shank, *Elect in the Son*, p. 16).

3. Methodists

"The free-will of man must have divine help in order that he may do good and please God" (Selecman, *Methodist Primer*, p. 32).

4. Presbyterian Church

Historically, the Presbyterians are basically Calvinistic and their Confession of Faith declares "that some men and angels are predestined to everlasting life, and others foreordained to everlasting death." In 1903, however, they added a statement which declares "that the doctrine of God's eternal decree is held in harmony with the doctrine of his love for all mankind,...that God is willing to bestow his saving grace on all who seek it...that men are responsible for their treatment of God's gracious offer, and no man is condemned except on the ground of his sin" (Miller, p. 59).

5. Disciples of Christ

Generally reject predestination.

6. Latter Day Saints

The third article of the thirteen "revealed" to Joseph Smith suggests that "all mankind may be saved, by obedience to the laws and ordinances of the gospel."

7. Jehovah's Witnesses

The Jehovah's Witnesses hold that all who will accept Christ can be saved but only 144,000 will actually go to heaven (*The Truth*, pp. 77-79).

8. Seventh-day Adventists

"On the one hand, Seventh-day Adventism teaches that man is dead in sin, and, therefore, even the initial promptings to a better life must come from God. On the other hand, it affirms 'that man is free to choose or reject the offer of salvation through Christ....' Putting these two statements together, we conclude that initial promptings to a better life must come, somehow, to every man, or at least to every man who hears the gospel, and that then man must make his own choice as to what he will do in response to these promptings. The decisive factor in determining who will be saved is thus not God's sovereign grace but man's free choice. The position of Seventh Day Adventism on this point would again appear to be basically the Arminian one" (Hoekema, p. 112).

9. Assemblies of God

The Assemblies of God do not believe that some men are predestined to be saved and others lost. "Predestination would limit Christ's atonement, and He died for all. It would nullify man's free will and amount to fatalism, which is gross error. Salvation is always for 'whosoever will'" (Riggs, p. 103).

10. Church of the Nazarene

"We believe that man's creation in Godlikeness included the ability to choose between right and wrong, and that thus he was made morally responsible; that through the fall of Adam he became depraved so that he cannot now turn and prepare himself by his own natural strength and works to faith and calling upon God. But we also believe that the grace of God through Jesus Christ is free, bestowed upon all men, enabling all who will to turn from sin to righteousness, believe on Jesus Christ for pardon and cleansing from sin, and follow good works pleasing and acceptable in his sight" (*Manual*, p. 29-30).

Teaching of the Scriptures on Predestination

The doctrine of "predestination" or "election" is much less of a vital question now than it was around 1800 when the Restoration Movement began. Then, *most denominations thought that only those individuals designated by God would be saved and all others lost.* God indicated His choice of those to be saved by giving them some kind of supernatural experience—a vision, tongues, the falling exercise, etc. Several key doctrines tied together: (1) only the elect could be saved; (2) the Holy Spirit came on one to tell him he was of the elect and to give him faith; (3) once a person was thus saved, he could not be lost.

Many denominations have changed their view and their practice. Even those whose creeds state a view of individual election often do not have such a view prevalent among their members.

The Bible does indeed speak of "predestination," but, as Shank explains it, Calvin taught that "the election to salvation is of particular men unconditionally, who comprise the corporate body incidentally." Biblical predestination, on the other hand, suggests "the election to salvation is corporate and comprehends individual men only in identification and association with the elect body" (Shank, p. 48).

III. The Scriptures

A. Inspiration and Authority

1. Roman Catholic

Ultimate authority for the Catholic rests, not in the Scriptures, but in the *church*. "The church has authority from God to teach regarding faith and morals, and in her teaching she is preserved from error by the special guidance of the Holy Ghost" (Gibbons, p. 54). "It will not suffice to tell me: We have an infallible scripture as a substitute for the infallible apostolate of the first century, for an infallible book is of no use to me without an infallible interpretor, as the history of Protestantism too clearly demonstrates" (Gibbons, p. 55). In Matthew 16:18, Gibbons says, Christ makes "a solemn prediction that no error shall ever invade His Church, and if she fell into error, the gates of hell have certainly prevailed against her" (p. 55).

"The church, as we have just seen, is the only Divinely constituted teacher of religion. Now, the Scripture is the great depository of the Word of God. Therefore, the church is the divinely appointed Custodian and Interpreter of the Bible. For, her office of infallible Guide were superfluous if each individual could interpret the Bible for himself" (Gibbons, p. 63). To the Catholic, then, the church, through its Pope, Cardinals, Bishops, and Priests is the "court" to give the correct interpretation of Scriptures. The word of the church, through the Pope, is binding and the Pope, when speaking on faith and morals, is infallible. Great weight is also given to tradition, to the way it has been done before, and to the actions of Councils.

Catholics, then, do regard the Bible as inspired and authoritative but only as it is interpreted by the church. Papal letters and tradition are also regarded as authoritative.

2. Baptist Church

"We believe that the Holy Bible was written by men divinely inspired, and is a perfect treasure of heavenly instruction; that it has God as its author, salvation for its end, and truth, without any mixture of error" (New Hampshire Confession of Faith; Wallace, p. 7). Baptists regard the Scriptures as the final authority although they do have "manuals" which explain their view of its meaning.

3. Methodists

Paragraph 65 of the Discipline states that "the Holy Scriptures contain all things necessary to salvation; so that whatsoever is not read therein, nor may be proved thereby, is not to be required of any man...." Methodists generally, however, take the Scriptures with less strictness than many of the more fundamental religions. They may, for example, give a statement by Paul or John less importance than a statement by Jesus and have been known to reject some statement of Scripture that does not agree with a belief they wish to hold. For many Methodists, "inspiration" does not mean absolute accuracy in bringing a message from God to men. In sum, they respect the Scriptures but do not generally follow them as strictly as more "fundamental" religions do.

4. Presbyterians

Generally, the Presbyterians regard the Bible as inspired and authoritative but they also have a "Confession of Faith" which states their beliefs. One of these statements says that the Scriptures " are given by inspiration of God," but continues, "our full persuasion and assurance of the infallible truth, and divine authority thereof, is from the inward work of the Holy Spirit, bearing witness by and with the word in our hearts" (Miller, p. 34).

Many Presbyterians, however, do not take a strict interpretation of Scripture, feeling that inspiration is more of the thought than of the words.

5. Disciples of Christ

The time was when the "Christian Church" took a position of carefully examining the Scriptures with the attempt to follow them closely. Since the more liberal element has taken precedence in the "Disciples of Christ," however, the appeal to Scripture is different. Like those in many denominations, Disciples of Christ frequently *do not look to the New Testament as an exact pattern*. Often they distinguish between Jesus and His apostles, giving more authority to Christ than the apostles. The fact that a passage declares the answer may not be taken as the end of the matter.

A typical statement from the Disciples of Christ today is found in Hampton Adams' *Why I Am A Disciple of Christ:* "From the very beginning of their movement, the Disciples have had a sound sense that the source of all that is to be learned about God's revelation in Christ is the New Testament. The fathers of the movement failed to appreciate the significance of the historic creeds of the church as a faithful effort to summarize faith. However, they were right in their contention that no Christian could stop his search for Christ at any historic creed but that he must get back to the New Testament itself.

"They did not have the means of Biblical interpretation that have been made increasingly effective by devout Biblical scholars since that day. Furthermore, their assumption that the New Testament intended to give an organized pattern to the church was naïve and unjustified. But their primary contention that the truth of God revealed in Christ must be appropriated from the Bible itself is supported by the scholarship of today with its emphasis on Biblical theology" (p. 100).

6. Latter Day Saints

Articles 8 and 9 of Joseph Smith's *Articles of Faith* state: "We believe the Bible to be the word of God as far as it is translated correctly; we also believe the Book of Mormon to be the word of God." They believe that revelation is not yet over but that "He will yet reveal many great and important things pertaining to the Kingdom of God" (Quoted in Gerstner, *The Theology of the Major Sects*, p. 51).

Mormons also accept *Doctrine and Covenants* and *Pearl of Great Price* as inspired Scripture. The *Book of Mormon* claims that the Catholic church took away from the gospel "many parts which are plain and most precious; and also many covenants of the Lord have they taken away" (I Nephi 13:26).

7. Jehovah's Witnesses

Authors of the Bible "did not write of their own impulse, but were inspired by God. 'Inspired' means that God 'moved these men by his own spirit or invisible empowering force, putting into their minds what they should write down as his 'word,' or message for mankind" (*Good News*, p. 14).

While the Jehovah's Witnesses regard the Bible as inspired and authoritative, they hold that the Witness Movement is the infallible interpreter of the Bible. "Nevertheless the Witness Movement has developed the role of the infallible interpreter of the infallible word. And, as with Romanism and all other groups which have yielded to this temptation, the infallible interpreter has tended to replace the infallible Word in the thinking and the faith of the believer. According to *The Watch Tower and Herald of Christ's Presence*, May, 1925, Russell was the angel referred to in Ezekiel 9:11, or the seventh messenger of the Church. That is clearly the notion of the infallible teacher. That Russell must have thought of himself in such a way, although he disclaimed 'superiority or supernatural power,' is apparent. How else can one explain his statement in *Studies in the Scriptures*, 'that it would be better to leave the Bible unread and read his *Studies* than to read the Bible and ignore his *Studies*? Rutherford, when he replaced Russell, said he spoke not his own words, but Jehovah's.

"So then, their nominal acceptance of the principle of an authoritative Scripture is vitiated by their practical acceptance of an infallible interpreter. The right of private judgment is, for all practical purposes, done away with, as the Witness bows to the hierarchy, or rather, the one at the head of the hierarchy" (Gerstner, pp. 34-35).

The Jehovah's Witnesses have made their own translation, *The New World Translation*, and prefer it above other translations because some of its variants favor their view such as in John 1:1— "and the word was *a* God."

8. Seventh-day Adventists

"Seventh-day Adventists hold the Protestant position that the Bible and the Bible only is the sole rule of faith and practice for Christians" (*Questions on Doctrine*, p. 28). They "do not regard the writings of Ellen G. White as an addition to the sacred canon of Scripture" and "do not think of them as of universal application, as in the Bible, but particularly for the Seventh-day Adventist Church" (*Questions on Doctrine*, p. 89).

It is strange that her writings come from a "spirit of prophecy" but are only for the Seventh-day Adventist Church. In their publications on doctrine such as in their new Bible Commentary, there is a section at the end of each chapter called "Ellen G. White Comments" (Martin, p. 580).

9. Assemblies of God

"The Holy Spirit of God is the divine author of the Bible, for these holy men of God spoke as they were moved of the Holy Ghost" (Riggs, p. 87).

"Every word is inspired in the original manuscripts" (Riggs, p. 88).

10. Church of the Nazarene

"We believe in the plenary inspiration of the Holy Scriptures, by which we understand the sixty-six books of the Old and New Testament given by divine inspiration, and inerrantly revealing the will of God concerning us in all things necessary to our salvation, so that whatever is not contained therein is not to be enjoined as an article of faith" (*Manual*, pp. 28-29).

Teaching of the Scripture on Religious Authority

Perhaps the most basic point of any religion is what it accepts as authority, and the differences in religion stem primarily from this point. If indeed the Catholic Church itself is the authority, then whatever it says is correct. If the *Book of Mormon* or Ellen G. White or the interpretations of the Watch Tower are authoritative, then whatever doctrines they propound are correct. If, as in some denominations one may decide for himself what Scriptures he wants to accept and which he would reject, then each individual is his own ultimate authority. The Bible, however, is the one and only source of God's revealed truth.

Consider the following:

1. *Either the Bible in its entirety is inspired and to be taken as authoritative or it should be rejected completely.* The basis of one's faith in any of the Bible would apply to it all. If God inspired a person in part of his writing, why not all of it? We are not at liberty to accept what we choose and reject what we choose. See II Timothy 3:16-17; II Peter 1:3; Jude 3; Galatians 1:6-12.

2. *Man is free to determine for himself what he understands the Scripture to mean, but he must also be ready to accept the results of his interpretation.* It is true that each is entitled to his own interpretation, but each will be approved or disapproved by his interpretation. Matthew 7:21 tells of those who thought they were followers of Christ who were rejected. Not all interpretations are equally good and only those which correspond with the original intent of God in revealing His Word will achieve in one's life what God intended. No one truly believes that "it does not matter what one believes so long as

he is sincere." Is it as good to believe atheism or communism as Christianity? Was Christ as pleased with Jezebel (Revelation 2:20) as with those who held fast His Word (Revelation 2:24-25)? Was Paul as pleased with those who taught another gospel as with those who followed his inspired message (Galatians 1:6-8)?

3. *To those who claim the need of modern revelation, the question must be asked, "What does your revelation provide for salvation that is not give in the Scriptures?"* None can answer. A way of emphasizing such a point is to draw a circle on a paper and ask what the *Book of Mormon* or other modern revelations provide that we need to be saved which is not in the Bible. If they could bring something forth, where would this leave all those who lived between the time the New Covenant began and their new revelation?

B. Relationship of the Testaments, 10 Commandments, Sabbath Day

1. Roman Catholic

The Catholics accept the Old and New Testaments as inspired and, in addition, also include in their Bible the books of the apocrypha which were written during the time between the Testaments. Portions are also added to certain other books such as Daniel and Esther. They use Old Testament passages and passages from apocryphal books as proof for doctrines to believe and practice today, apparently not making a proper distinction between the covenants. Gibbons, for example, writes "The same Divine precepts delivered through Moses to the Jews, on Mount Sinai, the same salutary warnings which the Prophets uttered throughout Judea, the same sublime and consoling lessons of morality which Jesus gave on the Mount—these are the lessons which the Church teaches from January till December" (Gibbons, p. 15).

2. Baptist Church

Like most denominations, *Baptists generally fail to make an adequate distinction between the Old and New Testaments.* They, for example, like to indicate that one may be saved today like "the thief on the cross," or that all should follow the ten commandments" (See Odle, *Church Members Handbook*, p. 21).

The following paragraphs also suggest this confusion:

"Christian believers are under a sacred obligation to hallow the Christian sabbath—all the force of past commandments is here concentrated. Only the form and day have changed; the substance remains. And as redemption is greater than the giving of the land of Canaan to a nation, so is the meaning of the sabbath greater to Christians than the old sabbath to the Hebrews. Their sabbath was to be different from other days. Our sabbath must be different from other days.

"The specific regulations of the Mosaic Law, for application in Palestine among an agricultural and pastoral people, do not apply in every instance to all our modern conditions in life; but the underlying principle applies, and we are guilty if we evade it. The Christian sabbath is a day for rest, for remembering God our Saviour Jesus Christ, for such employment and activities only as are in harmony with that great word of Christ, 'The Sabbath was made for man, and not man for the sabbath'" (Wallace, p. 105).

3. Methodist Church

In its *Discipline*, the Methodists also show *a lack of clear perception about what teachings of the Scripture are in force today*. Paragraph 66 of the *Discipline* states "The Old Testament is not contrary to the New; for both in the Old and New Testament everlasting life is offered to mankind by Christ, who is the only Mediator between God and man, being both God and Man. Wherefore they are not to be heard who feign that the old fathers did look only for transitory promises. Although the law given from God by Moses as touching ceremonies and rites doth not bind Christians, nor ought the civil precepts thereof of necessity be received in any commonwealth; yet notwithstanding, no Christian whatsoever is free from the obedience of the commandments which are called moral."

4. Presbyterian Church

"'The Law of God' is to guide us in the path of righteousness. God gave man his law and promised life if it was obeyed, and punishment and death if it was not obeyed. Man broke God's law and became the victim of sin. The law was still in force. It was made plain to Israel in the Ten Commandments which were given on Mount Sinai, setting forth briefly man's duty to God and man. To the moral law were added the ceremonial laws to guide in worship. These ceremonial laws foreshadowed Christ and the way of forgiveness and restoration through him, so that, since the saving work of Christ, the ceremonial laws of the Old Testament are no longer observed by the Church. The people of Israel received also judicial laws to guide them in the body politic. These laws are no longer binding, except as they are supported by their evident justice. The moral law, however, is still binding" (Miller, p. 64).

5. Disciples of Christ

Coming out of the Restoration Movement where the distinction between the covenants was clearly established, the point should be clear. In defending instrumental music, however, appeal will often be made to Old Testament worship.

6. Latter Day Saints

Doctrine and Covenants (84:57) declares that the *Book of Mormon* is "the new covenant" (also see 1:17-22). Such passages indicate that Joseph Smith and the *Book of Mormon* ushered in a "new covenant" but not to the exclusion of the Bible (42:12). There does not seem to be any clear statement distinguishing between the covenants of Moses and Christ, and their use of the Aaronic Priesthood is evidence of confusion on this point.

7. Jehovah's Witnesses

"Since God has taken the Jewish law covenant with its Ten Commandments out of the way by nailing it to the torture stake on which Jesus died, the Christians must observe, not the law-covenant shadows, but the reality" (*Let God Be True*, p. 177). "His coming to fulfill such Law and the Prophets proves that the law covenant and the sabbath obligations are not binding upon his disciples" (*Let God Be True*, p. 175).

8. Seventh-day Adventists

On pages 130-131 of *Questions on Doctrine*, the Adventists present their theory of the *division of the Mosaical law into "moral" and "ceremonial" elements*. The ten commandments are called "moral" law and these, they say, are still in force. As proof of this, they offer James 2:12 which says we shall be judged by the law; Romans 3:31 which, they say, establishes the decalogue in the Christian faith; and Romans 7:14 which declares the law to be "spiritual."

They argue that, while the ceremonial law about sacrifices and social life is taken away, the moral precepts of the ten commandments remain, including the fourth one to keep the Sabbath.

Their arguments in favor of keeping the Sabbath include:

a. God hallowed the seventh day—Genesis 2:2-3.
b. The Israelites kept the Sabbath before the Law of Moses was given—Exodus 16:23-30.
c. Keeping the Sabbath was one of the ten commandments (Exodus 20:8) and is still in force along with the other moral commandments.
d. Jesus kept the Sabbath and was called "Lord of the Sabbath" (Mark 2:27-28).
e. Paul kept the Sabbath (Acts 17:2).
f. The disciples met on the Sabbath (Acts 20:7, NEB)
g. Ellen G. White received a revelation emphasizing the need to restore keeping the Sabbath.

h. "We believe that the restoration of the Sabbath is indicated in the Bible prophecy of Revelation 14:9-12. Sincerely believing this, we regard the observance of the Sabbath as a test of our loyalty to Christ as Creator and Redeemed" (*Questions on Doctrine*, p. 153; see also pp. 183 and 190).

9. Assemblies of God

"Christians are not under the Old Testament law but are saved and kept by grace through grace through faith." "Does this free Christians from keeping the Old Testament law? Yes, except where that law is repeated in the New Testament." Ephesians 2:8; Romans 6:14.

10. Church of the Nazarene

"We believe that the scriptural method of gathering money for the support of the church is by means of tithes and offerings. We urge that our people adopt tithing as the scriptural and satisfactory plan, that each member may do his minimum share in support of the whole church, local, district, and general" (*Manual*, p. 47). In the *Manual*, the Old and New Testaments are said to reveal "the will of God concerning us in all things necessary to our salvation" (*Manual*, p. 28). It appears, then, that a clear statement on the relationship of a Christian to the Old Testament is lacking.

Teaching of the Scripture on the Old and New Testaments and on Keeping the Sabbath

1. *The entire Bible is equally inspired and, thus, is the Word of God* (I Peter 1:21; Hebrews 1:1; II Timothy 3:15-16; John 16:13; Galatians 1:6-12). In II Peter 3:15-16, Peter calls Paul's writings Scripture, thus confirming that New Testament writings are also considered as Scriptures.

2. *Not every teaching or command in the Bible was intended to apply to every person in every circumstance.* Noah alone was told to build an ark

(Genesis 6:14); Abram and his family alone were told to leave their home for another country (Genesis 12:1); Moses alone was commanded to go to Egypt to release the children of Israel (Exodus 3:10); Jesus told His apostles to wait in Jerusalem for the baptism of the Holy Spirit (Acts 1:4-5); the Israelites alone were given the law of Moses and it was never given to Gentiles (Exodus 19:3-6; Romans 3:1-2; Acts 15:28-29).

3. *The covenant God made with the Israelites through Moses not only was never intended to be a law for Gentiles but once Christ came, it no longer applied even to Jews.* Hebrews 7:11-28 explains the change of priesthood and the change of the covenant. Hebrews 8:6-13 tells of the former law in "ordinances" being taken away; II Corinthians 3:1-11 tells of the "ministration of death, written and engraven on stones" which is passing away. Galatians 5:4 says those who seek to be justified by the law "are fallen away from grace."

4. *That there is no division between "moral" and "ceremonial" aspects of the law of Moses is clear,* not only from the foregoing passages but also from Romans 7:1-8 which declares that we are discharged from the law which said "thou shalt not covet."

5. *As to the Sabbath as still being in force,* note the following:

   a. While God hallowed the seventh day, He nowhere stated that it would perpetually be the prescribed day of worship for His people.

   b. While the Law of Moses declared the seventh day to be special, no one, neither Jew nor Gentile, is now under that law. Even those who claim to keep the sabbath as commanded in the Law do not follow the commands given there about how to keep it—don't gather sticks, don't build a fire, don't travel over three-fourths of a mile from the city wall, etc. How could the law be binding if the means of keeping it are not?

   c. Jesus kept the Sabbath because He lived under the Law which was in force until He died (Hebrews 9:16-17). Paul did not keep the Sabbath after his conversion but did meet with Jews who were assembling on that day.

d. Acts 20:7 should be translated "first day of the week" even though in those times, a day began at sundown rather than midnight.

e. Although the New Covenant contains restatements or additional emphasis on nine of the ten commandments, there is no teaching of the observance of the Sabbath after Pentecost. In fact, Paul says no man is to judge us in keeping the Sabbath (Colossians 2:16-17).

f. The following passages show that it was the first day rather than the seventh day which was special to Christians: John 20:1, 19, 26; Acts 20:7; I Corinthians 16:1; Revelation 1:10 speaks of the "Lord's Day" which, according to early church writers, was the first day of the week.

g. Early writers such as the Epistle of Barnabas (A.D. 100), Epistles of Ignatius (A.D. 107), Justin Martyr (A.D. 145), Dionysius (A.D. 170), Clement of Alexandria (A.D. 174), Tertullian (A.D. 200), Origen (A.D. 230) all say that the first day was the day for Christian worship and communion. (See Gerstner, pp. 24-26, and Douty, *Another Look and Seventh-day Adventism*, Chapter VI.)

IV. Salvation

A. Roman Catholic

As explained earlier, *Catholics believe in original sin. Babies*, who have original sin but no actual sins, need baptism to cleanse them from original sin or they will go to *limbo*, a state not as good as heaven but not as bad as hell. *Adults*, on the other hand, need to be justified from both original and actual sin.

Gibbons says that "Baptism is the essential means established for washing away the stain of original sin and the door by which we find admittance to His Church" (p. 221). "Baptism also clothes us with the *garment of sanctity*, so that our soul becomes a fit dwelling place for the Holy Ghost" (p. 227). *Baptism* may be administered by immersion, affusion (pouring water on the candidate), or by sprinkling (p. 228).

"For an adult sinner the conditions necessary for the lawful reception of baptism are faith and repentance. Let us explain our terms. By an adult sinner we mean one who, in addition to inheriting original sin, has also been guilty of actual sin. By faith we do not, obviously, mean the virtue of faith possessed as a principle of activity arising from habitual grace (for baptism is the means to his habitual grace), but simply an act of faith to which the aspirant to baptism is assisted by actual graces from God, preparing and disposing him for the habitual grace that is to come from baptism. By repentance we mean that, in the case of the actual sinner, the renunciation of Satan must inevitably include contrition for the actual sins of which he has been guilty" (Smith, *The Teaching of the Catholic Church*, p. 792). Smith goes on to state, however, that if one's repentance is not genuine, it "would make the reception unlawful, but it would not invalidate it" (p. 793). The baptism, thus, would do no good until the person should later repent but he would not have to be baptized again (pp. 793-794).

Smith also says that, while priests ordinarily should baptize, that so long as one uses water, has the proper intent, and the proper words are spoken, then the baptism is considered valid (p. 788). Catholics *do not accept* the view that *once a person is saved he cannot be lost*. Smith says, "Sanctifying grace is lost by mortal sin" (p. 530).

B. Baptist Church

Baptists believe that *justification is by "faith only,"* suggesting that when one "takes Jesus Christ as the object of his faith, puts his trust in him wholly" he has done his part to receive God's gift of salvation. Their definition of faith, however, includes a spirit of obedience and repentance from sin (Wallace, p. 40-41). This process also is called regeneration or the "new birth." Being a "born again" Christian means that one has experienced a time of emotional as well as intellectual commitment. This means a direct action of the Holy Spirit to give one a personal sense of being saved. "Except by the act of the Holy Spirit, there can be no New Birth" (Wallace, p. 47).

This rebirth is not usually called baptism of the Holy Spirit, however, "The repentance which is inseparably linked with faith and leads to salvation is godly sorrow for sin, such a sorrow as can arise only when the Holy Spirit has moved upon the heart" (Wallace, p. 52). "Unless the soul is incited to use its powers, seek the Saviour, and forsake sin, there will be no decision, no repentance, no faith. Hence, the need of prayer to God that the Holy Spirit shall stir to action as well as to give light and power" (Wallace, p. 54).

The Baptists correctly consider sanctification as not just cleansing at the time of the new birth but as a continuing process. *"Regeneration is the beginning of sanctification—It is no more than the beginning." It is not sanctification. By regeneration a man becomes a new creature, but not a completed spiritual creation* (Wallace, p. 67).

"The Holy Spirit, when he regenerates a human soul, does not retire as though he had completed his work....It is his to be active still in the heart of the believer, continuing his life-giving work, until he can present the soul without spot or wrinkle or any such thing" (Wallace, p. 68).

Baptists believe in the *perseverance of the saints or* "once saved, always saved." This view stems from their Calvinistic background and was, at one time, the natural companion of the doctrine of predestination. Now their view is that the one who is truly saved "will not" fall. Anyone who falls away is said not to have had "saving faith" in the beginning (Wallace, pp. 74-76). The New Hampshire Confession of Faith, to which Baptists subscribe, states it this way, "We believe that such only are real believers as endure unto the end; that their persevering attachment to Christ is the grand mark which distinguishes them from superficial professors; that a special Providence watches over their welfare; and that they are kept by the power of God through faith unto salvation" (Wallace, p. 74).

Scriptures cited for this view are John 3:31; 1 John 2:19; Romans 8:28; Philippians 1:6; 2:12-13.

Baptists teach *baptism* as an ordinance of the church to which one must submit before he can be accepted into the Baptist Church. Since one is saved before baptism, he is, therefore, saved *before* he is baptized into the Baptist Church. Wallace says, for example, "Unless his baptism represents his own faith in Christ and expresses his passing from death to life, it is vain and void. Until the man has been regenerated by the Holy Spirit and voluntarily enters upon the life of obedience to Christ's commands, he is not fit to be baptized" (p. 94).

Baptists believe only in *baptism by immersion* and *do not baptize infants.*

C. Methodists

Paragraph 69 of the *Discipline* states: "We are accounted righteous before God only for the merit of our Lord and Saviour Jesus Christ, by faith, and not for our own works or deservings. Wherefore, that we are justified by faith only is a most wholesome doctrine, and very full of comfort."

A similar statement from Selecman is, "Those who truly repent and believe on the Lord Jesus Christ are born again. This is called the *new birth, regeneration,* or *conversion.* Emphasis is laid on surrender to Christ leading to transformation" (pp. 33-34).

Methodists regard *sanctification* as a "renewal of our fallen nature by the Holy Ghost," a removal of guilt, and the power "to love God with all our hearts and to walk in His Holy commandments blameless" (p. 86).

Methodists do not believe in *"once saved, always saved."* One can "fall into sin after justification." After receiving the Holy Spirit, "we may depart from grace given, and fall into sin, and, by the grace of God, rise again and amend our lives" (*Discipline*, p. 72).

D. Presbyterians

"But sincere believers receive not only justification by faith in Jesus Christ and the privileges of children of God through adoption; they also receive sanctification an inner transformation which leads to victory over sin. The process of sanctification, however, is not complete in this life, for there is the conflict with evil in the heart and in the life, but by the work of God's Spirit believers are at last made perfect in holiness."

Miller defines faith as a word which involves "hearing the message of the gospel," "belief in the truth of the message of the Scriptures," and "the act of accepting, receiving, and resting upon Christ alone for salvation." He continues: "Associated with faith is repentance, consciousness of sinfulness and unworthiness, awareness of the righteousness of God and his law, a sense of the mercy of God in Christ, sincere sorrow for wrongdoing, and the purpose to live as God would have us live." "We are saved by faith in Jesus Christ, not by anything that we do, for we can do nothing sufficiently good to earn salvation, but by obedience to God's commandments the believer shows his gratitude to God, sets an example to others, and glorifies God."

"The Presbyterian Confession holds that 'once saved, always saved.' In other words, God will not forsake anyone who has truly turned to Christ in faith. However, because of the sinfulness that still lurks in the heart, and because of the temptations of this world, they may fall into sin, even grievous sins, and displease God and grieve the Holy Spirit. But this is only for a time and in the end the grace of God will be victorious" (Miller, pp. 62-63).

E. Disciples of Christ

Unlike those in the Restoration Movement of the 1800's, current Disciples of Christ *do not regard baptism as an essential prerequisite for forgiveness of sins.* Their growing practice of open membership, "receiving unimmersed Christians from other denominations into full membership of a Disciples of Christ Church," could hardly be consistent with a view that baptism is for remission of sins since such is not the practice of denominations generally (Adams, pp.

46-47). For persons not coming from another denomination, Disciples "practice believer's baptism by immersion." *Infants* are not baptized (Adams, p. 48).

The Disciples *do not believe in "once saved, always saved."*

F. Latter Day Saints

The statements by various Mormon authors do not all present the same view about salvation. In *Look* magazine, October 5, 1954, for example, Evans writes "Mormons believe in universal salvation that all men will be saved, but each one in his own order." Yet, in Article 3 of Smith's *Articles of Faith*, he says, "We believe that through the Atonement of Christ, all mankind may be saved, by obedience to the laws and ordinances of the Gospel." Article 4 goes on to say "We believe that the first principles and ordinances of the Gospel are: (1) Faith in the Lord Jesus Christ; (2) Repentance; (3) Baptism by immersion for the remission of sins; (4) Laying on of hands for the gift of the Holy Ghost." The *Book of Mormon*, Moroni 8:11 states: "And their little children need no repentance neither baptism. Behold, baptism is unto the remission of sins." Mormon practice, then, requires faith, repentance, and baptism by immersion for remission of sins. Yet, *Doctrine and Covenants* 20:37 says, "All those who...truly manifest by their works that they have received of the Spirit of Christ unto the remission of their sins, shall be received by baptism into His church."

Baptism for the dead is taught by Mormons from such passages as *Doctrine and Covenants* 124:1-16 and 1 Corinthians 15:29, and it is practiced regularly. Careful genealogical tables are developed so that persons can be baptized for their ancestors as well as for famous persons of the past. Yet, in Alma 34:32-35, the *Book of Mormon* teaches that "this life is the time for men to prepare to meet God; yea, behold the day of this life is the day for men to perform their labors....For until death, behold. Ye have become subjected to the spirit of the devil, and he doth seal you his."

Although Mormons teach "faith, repentance, and baptism by immersion for remission of sins" their view of the nature of the Trinity brings into question whether they truly baptize into "the name of the Father, Son, and Holy Spirit." (For discussion of this topic, see Joe Ed Furr, "Is Mormon Baptism Valid," *Firm Foundation* [May 17, 24, and 31] XCIV, Nos. 20, 21, 22.)

Mormons *do not believe in "once saved, always saved";* rather, they suggest that one must demonstrate "endurance to the end in keeping the commandments of God" (McConkie, *What the Mormons Think of Christ*, p. 28; quoted in Martin, p. 194).

G. Jehovah's Witnesses

"How can you respond to this love of God? You can do so by presenting yourself in dedication to Jehovah, to become his willing slave.—Romans 12:11…You must repent of whatever part you have had in the immoralities, the politics, and the wars of the 'present wicked system of things.' (Galatians 1:3, 4)…Then, after repenting and turning around, you may dedicate yourself in prayer to Jehovah to become his 'slave,' on the basis of your faith in Jesus' sacrifice, and then symbolize this dedication of yourself by receiving Christian baptism" (*Good News*, pp. 179-181). According to this teaching, *baptism* "is not a washing away of one's sins, because cleansing from sin comes only through faith in Jesus Christ (Ephesians 1:7). Rather, it is a public demonstration, testifying that one has made a solemn dedication to Jehovah God…" (*The Truth*, p. 183-184).

Sanctification is regarded as a continuing process in which a member of Christ's body "must be set apart more and more from this world and to the holy service of Jehovah God, demonstrating their dependability by carrying out their dedication faithfully until death" (*Let God Be True*, p. 301). Jehovah's Witnesses *do not believe in the impossibility of apostasy*. "To turn back would mark them as agreement-breakers" (*Let God Be True*, p. 302).

H. Seventh-day Adventists

Basically, Seventh-day Adventists teach salvation by *"faith only"* as do some other groups already studied. In *Questions on Doctrine*, for example, they say "that which saves is grace alone, through faith in the living Christ" (p. 102). "When we accept Him [Christ], we are justified" (p. 387). "The first work of grace is justification," but, "the continuing work of grace is sanctification" (p. 410).

The *Seventh-day Adventist Church Manual*, p. 57, states that baptism is a public expression of both faith in Christ and forgiveness of sins. They teach *baptism by immersion* and *reject infant baptism*. They do not believe in *perseverance of the saints* stating that if a righteous man turns back to sin, "he forfeits all the blessings of salvation and goes down to death" (*Questions on Doctrine*, p. 415; see also Hoekema, p. 133).

I. Assemblies of God

"The Holy Spirit convicts of sin, grants repentance, and imparts everlasting life. It is thus by grace we are saved—not of works but through faith in God." Man's part is to "receive a love for the truth (II Thessalonians 2:10), must believe the gospel (Mark 16:16) and must receive Christ into the heart (John 1:12, 13)" (Riggs, p. 105). "Salvation is received through repentance toward God and faith toward the Lord Jesus Christ" (*Statement of Fundamental Truths*, p. 7).

Sanctification is a continuing work that continues after justification as the new man takes the place of the old (Riggs, pp. 107-108). *Baptism* is a "public confession of discipleship and a symbol of the death, burial, and resurrection which has taken place in their [new converts'] hearts" (Riggs, p. 117). Baptism is by *immersion* only (Riggs, p. 117).

Baptism of the Holy Spirit is taught as following one's acceptance by Christ. "One may receive baptism in the Spirit by being a Christian in the first place (John 14:17), by asking the Father (Luke 11:13), and by believing on Jesus (John 7:39), and by obeying God (Acts 5:32)."

Speaking in tongues will evidence one's Holy Spirit baptism. Other gifts are also given (Riggs, p. 114).

Those once saved can be lost (Riggs, p. 111).

J. Church of the Nazarene

"We believe that repentance, which is a sincere and thorough change of the mind in regard to sin, involving a sense of personal guilt and a voluntary turning away from sin is demanded of all who have by act or purpose become sinners against God. The Spirit of God gives to all who will repent the gracious help of penitence of heart and hope of mercy, that they may believe unto pardon and spiritual life.

"We believe that justification is that gracious and judicial act of God, by which He grants full pardon of all guilt and complete release from the penalty of sins committed, and acceptance as righteous, to all who believe on Jesus Christ and receive Him as Lord and Saviour.

"We believe that regeneration, or the new birth, is that gracious work of God whereby the moral nature of the repentant believer is spiritually quickened and given a distinctively spiritual life, capable of faith, love, and obedience....

"We believe that justification, regeneration, and adoption are simultaneous in the experience of seekers after God and are obtained upon the condition of faith, preceded by repentance; and that to this work and state of grace the Holy Spirit bears witness.

"We believe that entire sanctification is that act of God, subsequent to regeneration, by which believers are made free from original sin, or depravity, and brought into a state of entire devotement to God, and the holy obedience of love made perfect" (*Manual*, pp. 30-31).

"We believe that Christian baptism is a sacrament signifying acceptance of the benefits of the atonement of Jesus Christ, to be administered to believers as declarative of their faith in Jesus Christ as their Saviour, and full purpose of obedience in holiness and righteousness.

"Baptism being the symbol of the New Testament, young children may be baptized, upon request of parents or guardians who shall give assurance for them of necessary Christian training.

"Baptism may be administered by sprinkling, pouring, or immersion, according to the choice of the applicant" (*Manual*, p. 33).

Teaching of the Scriptures on Salvation

1. Ephesians 2:8-10 teaches that we are saved by grace through faith—*grace* summarizing God's part and *faith* summarizing man's part. Ephesians, Romans, Galatians, and other books use salvation by faith as a contrast to salvation by *law*. The difference is that under the *law system, perfection was required*—either do everything right or receive the punishment for violating the law. In this case, man, by his own righteousness might earn salvation. An opposite view to "salvation by works" would be a system in which *man did nothing*. Such was the view of the strict Calvinist who said that sal-

vation was by faith alone and God gave man the faith. Such a view makes man completely passive.

Salvation by faith, on the other hand, "is a system by which *man does something* to indicate he wishes to come to God and then God gives His grace to cover man's sins. This allows the undeserved punishment for sin which Christ received on the cross to be applied to the spiritual account of those who have met the conditions set forth to receive it. *Such a plan does not require perfection* as does "salvation by works," but it does require that one who wishes to receive the benefits of Christ's death should *demonstrate* his desire to share in Christ's sacrifice.

Such an explanation is the only way to reconcile all the teaching of the New Testament on salvation. Hebrews 5:9 says Christ "became unto all them that *obey* him the author of eternal salvation" and Matthew 7:21 says only those who do the will of the Father will enter the kingdom of heaven. James 2:24 says justification is by *works* and I Peter 3:21 says *baptism* saves us. Other passages, at the same time, suggest that we are saved by *faith, not works* (Romans 3:28; 4:1-5; 5:1). All of these statements are seen in *harmony*, however, when we recognize that man cannot meet a perfect standard, thereby earning or meriting his salvation. This does not mean, however, that God gives him everything. *God gives man grace but asks him to "lay hold" on this gift through certain acts of obedience which man can do.*

2. Being saved from past sins or *justification* comes when a person believes in Christ as God's Son, *repents* of his sins, publically *confesses his faith*, and *submits to baptism for remission of sins*. Most who discuss differences on this question fall into the useless practice of one person quoting scriptures that speak *only of faith* while the other quotes *only passages that require baptism*. Such is futile. Acts 16:31 speaks only of faith and I Peter 3:21 only of baptism but neither verse proves that only faith or only baptism is required. There must be some view which properly relates both faith and baptism. *All* who call themselves Christians regard *faith* as essential and all, likewise, regard *baptism* as being a beneficial practice.

No one is opposed to either. The basic question is whether initial forgiveness of sins and beginning of the new life comes *before* or *after* baptism. Some teach, for example, that one is saved the instant he believes, and they often express their doctrine by stating that "salvation is by faith only." Another group will say, "No, a person is saved when he has believed and repented." Still another may say, "One is not actually born again until he has believed, repented, and been baptized."

Which is the *final* act of obedience in accepting God's offer to become a child of His? At what point in obedience should one consider himself to be free from past sin and born into the family? Galatians 3:27: "For as many of you as were *baptized into Christ*." This verse makes it very clear that it is with baptism that a person is placed "into Christ," where all spiritual blessings such as salvation and eternal life are to be found (Ephesians 1:3). I Corinthians 12:13: "For in one Spirit were we all *baptized into one body*." Again it is clear that baptism is the act with which one is placed into the body of Christ. In Romans 6:4 we find with which act one starts to live the *new life*: "We were buried therefore with him through *baptism* into death: that like as Christ was raised from the dead through the glory of the Father, so we also might walk in *newness of life*." Walking in the new life starts when? *After baptism!* Acts 2:41 adds its testimony to the same conclusion for it tells just when those who heard Peter's sermon on Pentecost were considered a part of the disciples. "They then that received his word were baptized: and there were *added [unto them]* in that day about three thousand souls." When they had progressed through baptism, they were then considered Christians, part of the church. Acts 2:38, likewise, places "forgiveness of sins" *after* a believer repents and is baptized.

Finally, in Acts 22:16 we read a statement of Ananias made to Paul at the direct request of the Lord. Paul's *faith*, as all agree, began on the road to Damascus. He had already been praying and fasting for three days, definite evidence of *repentance*. Yet the messenger of the Lord tells him, "arise, and be baptized, and wash away thy sins." Here is a man who had already believed and has already repented, but who is still guilty of his sins. But *with baptism*, says Ananias, his sins will be "washed away." To say that one today loses his past sins *before* he reaches the point of baptism is to offer a way of salvation not open to Paul or any other New Testament convert.

Now we know when it is that a person is put "into Christ," "saved" from past sins, and made a "new creature" to walk in a new life—when he *completes the process as far as baptism*.

Jesus, of course, expressed this very view in Mark 16:16 where He said, "He that believeth and is baptized shall be saved." Those believing one is saved by faith only will often counter, however, with verse 17 as if it negates verse 16: "He that disbelieveth shall be condemned." It does not say, they maintain, that "He that disbelieveth and is not baptized shall be condemned." Such reasoning, clearly, is a misuse of the passage. Jesus first states *the positive*: believe and be baptized to be saved. The, He tells what happens to one *who does not believe*—he is condemned. *But what of the one who believes and is not baptized?* The verse does not consider him except he certainly is not included in the positive statement of one who will be saved. What verse would speak to the condition of one who believes but has not been baptized? "But wilt thou know, O vain man, that faith apart from works is barren....Ye see that by works a man is justified, and not only by faith" (James 2:20, 24). James is not contradicting Paul for James is not speaking of "works of the law" or "meritorious works." Rather, he is speaking of *acts of obedience* which grow from faith. Until faith has been expressed in action, such as baptism, it is fruitless and, in James' words, is dead.

The major difference regarding conversion among prominent religious bodies in the United States, then, is not so much a difference on *what* the biblical commands are, but a difference on just *when* on is added to the body of Christ and thus made a part of the "saved" or kingdom. As we have seen, conversion is the process of getting "into Christ." With *belief* one starts toward Christ by placing his trust in Him, and this faith is evidenced by a public confession. With *repentance* he moves still closer to Christ as he remakes his life after the pattern Christ gave. With *baptism* he buries the old life and is raised alive "in Christ." Baptism is the funeral for the old man and the birth of the new.

3. *Holy Spirit baptism* plays no part in one's being saved from past sins. This view developed when many believed in predestination. If God chose who would be saved, then He needed some *means of notifying them they were of the elect.* This, they said, was done when God sent the Holy Spirit on the elect. Testifying of this experience was regarded as a means by which one could demonstrate to others he was saved and thus to be accepted for church membership.

Today, even many who no longer believe in predestination still view Holy Spirit baptism as part of the conversion process. *If the Holy Spirit must come on one to save him, however, does not this still make God to choose some to be saved and others lost?*

Holy Spirit baptism came only twice in the Scriptures—once on Pentecost for the Jews and once at the house of Cornelius for the Gentiles. Acts 1:5; 10:44-46; and 11:15-18 link these two events. Had this happened more than these two times during the first ten years of the church, Peter would not have explained it as he did.

Had an "experience" such as Paul had on the road to Damascus been sufficient to take away sin, Ananias would not have told Paul later to "wash away" his sins (Acts 22:16).

4. *Sanctification* in the Scriptures sometimes refers to the cleansing that comes at the time of baptism. In writing to the Corinthians, for example, Paul speaks of the time they were washed, sanctified, and justified as the same (I Corinthians 6:11). The term sanctification also may apply to continuing to live a clean or holy life (I Thessalonians 4:3). As we "walk in the light," we are cleansed (I John 1:7). There is nothing in the Scripture, however, which suggests sanctification to mean some special time of cleansing coming after baptism.

5. *The Scriptures clearly do not teach that once a person has been saved from past sins at baptism that he "cannot" be lost or that he "will not" be lost.* Simon is described by the Bible as having been a believer who was baptized; yet he sinned and was told he would *"perish,"* that he was in the *"gall of bitterness"* and the *"bond of iniquity"* and that *"his heart was not right with God."* That his first faith was valid is clear from the instructions Peter gave him—repent and pray. If his initial salvation had not been acceptable, he would have been told so (Acts 8:20-24).

    On almost every page of the New Testament there are *warnings of falling away.* In fact, the only time the phrase "fall from grace" is used in the Bible is Galatians 5:4 which says "ye are fallen away from grace." Other passages to use on this point are: Hebrews 6:4-6; 10:26-27; Revelation 2:4-7; 3:5, 14-22; II Peter 2:20-22; Galatians 1:8; I Corinthians 10:1-12. Note how in these passages some mention is made of *a right relationship to God and then, after sin, that relationship is changed.*

    The one who "has tasted" or "has received a knowledge of the truth," or "has escaped the defilements of the world," commits sins and now is in a condition of being *lost* unless he repents.

    There is, of course, *some security for the believer.* Satan cannot take him away against his will and God can keep until the end those whose faith is strong. I John 1:7 says that "if we walk in the light, as he is in the light" then Christ will continue to cleanse our sins. It is not a question of either believing that the saved cannot be lost or that those in Christ must live in constant fear. The truth lies in another alternative—"knowing Him whom we have believed" and trusting Him to keep us until that day while also knowing that we must "be faithful unto death" (II Timothy 1:12; Revelation 2:10).

V. The Church

A. Roman Catholic

1. Catholics regard the church as the *one body* of Christ and reject the idea of many branches or denominations. Gibbons says, "We must conclude that it never was His intention to establish or to sanction various conflicting denominations, but one corporate body, with all the members united under one visible Head; for as the church is a visible body, it must have a visible head" (p. 5). He continues, "With all due respect for my dissenting brethren, truth compels me to say that this unity of doctrine and government is not to be found in the Protestant sects, taken collectively or separately" (p. 7).

   Catholics like to point out that since the Protestant denominations sprang from the Catholic Church and since they carried with them some of the traditions which developed over the years in Catholicism, that if the Catholics are wrong, then so are the Protestants; and if the Catholics are right, then the Protestants are also wrong.

2. The *organization* of the Catholic Church is well known. "The faithful of each Parish are subject to their immediate Pastor. Each Pastor is subordinate to his Bishop, and each Bishop of Christendom acknowledges the jurisdiction of the Bishop of Rome, the successor of St. Peter, and Head of the Catholic Church" (Gibbons, p. 9). The visible head of the Catholic Church, then, is the Pope who has cardinals, archbishops, bishops, and priests reporting to him.

3.   *Membership* in the Catholic Church is dependent upon baptism as a means of "washing away the stain of original sin" and "the door by which we find admittance into His church." Pius XII stated "only those are to be accounted really members of the Church who have been regenerated in the waters of Baptism and profess the true faith, and have not cut themselves off from the structure of the Body by their own unhappy act or been severed there-from…" (quoted in Smith, p. 706). The Catholic Church teaches "the necessity of belonging to the Catholic Church in order to obtain salvation" (Smith, p. 708.)

4.   The Catholic Church ordains *priests* to dispense grace and to fill duties as successors of the Apostles (Gibbons, p. 317). According to Gibbons, the Priest is a preacher and one who administers the sacraments such as baptism, the communion, confession, extreme unction, etc. Since 1123, priests have been refused the privilege of marriage and the explanation given that the celibate or unmarried state was superior. Under growing pressure in the last few years, it appears that the Catholic Church may be weakening on this point.

5.   At the Council of Nicea in 325, a creed was written which stated, "I believe in the One, Holy, Catholic, and Apostolic Church." From this the Catholic Church has drawn its *name*, "Catholic," which means "universal." "Roman" comes from the time of the split into the Eastern (Greek) and Western (Roman) churches.

B. Baptist Church

1.   Since Baptists think that a person is saved when he *believes* in Christ and that this happens *apart from church membership*, they have to accept as fact that *there are saved persons in all churches*. They regard themselves as a denomination and consider church membership as a matter separate and apart from salvation. While they require that anyone coming to them from another denomination be immersed if he has not been so baptized earlier, they do not regard an unbaptized person as unsaved.

2.   The Baptist Church is *congregationally organized* with each local unit being its own authority. Baptists says "that the action of each local

congregation is final" (Pendleton, *Baptist Church Manual*, p. 112). Each Baptist Church has a pastor and deacons. By pastor, they refer to the minister even though they cite the references to the qualifications of elders or bishops as applying to him. While recognizing that the terms "elder," "bishop," and "pastor" refer to the same office, they state that the work of a pastor is "the administration of the ordinances as well as the preaching of the word" (Pendleton, p. 26). The Baptist Church recognizes the priesthood of all believers and has no especially-designated priests. The Baptist Church has associations in which local churches work together but they prefer to call the representatives "messengers" rather than "delegates" and deny that the association has authority over an individual church.

3. "It is most likely that in the Apostolic age when there was but 'one Lord, one faith, and one baptism,' and no differing denominations existed, the baptism of a convert by that very act constituted him a member of the church, and at once endowed him with all the rights and privileges of full membership. In that sense, 'baptism was the door into the church.' Now it is different; and while churches are desirous of receiving members, they are wary and cautious that they do not received unworthy persons. The churches, therefore, have candidates come before them, make their statement, give their 'experience,' and then their reception is decided by a vote of the members. And while they cannot become members without baptism, yet it is the vote of the body which admits them to its fellowship on receiving baptism" (Hiscox, *The Standard Manual for Baptist Churches*, p. 22).

4. Baptists generally claim to be able to trace their existence back through history to the original church of the New Testament and, thus, claim that Christ was their founder. They admit, of course, that many of the groups in their "chain" differed from each other and from present-day Baptists in their beliefs, but suggest that they did hold certain key doctrines in common such as a reliance on the Scriptures, rejection of the Roman Catholic apostasy, and baptism by immersion. "Denying the orthodoxy of the Romish

Church, they rebaptized persons received from that body, and hence were called Anabaptists" (Hiscox, p. 158). "Ana" means again. This term "Anabaptist" eventually was shortened into "Baptist," and is appropriate because of the emphasis the Baptists place on the requirement for immersion as a prerequisite to membership in their denomination.

C. Methodist Church

1. Selecman quotes Dr. Gilbert T. Rowe as saying: "Finally, as among Protestants, Methodism stands for an inclusive Christianity. It believes that the things that unite Christians are far more important than the things that divide. It has no exclusive doctrines, rites, or ceremonies." Selecman continues, "It teaches that all men are included in the atonement and the gospel invitation; that all must repent and believe on the Lord Jesus Christ; that all followers of Christ may have access to the sacraments of baptism and the Lord's Supper; and that ordination by any established evangelical church is valid. A letter from any Christian church may be accepted as the only condition of membership" (Selecman, p. 36). Thus, Methodists accept the *denominational view* and consider themselves one among many Protestant sects.

2. Methodists are governed primarily through a series of *conferences* ranging from the General Conference which meets every four years and which is described as "the one law-making body," through Jurisdictional, Annual, District, Quarterly, and Church Conferences. Methodists have *bishops* elected by the Jurisdictional Conference which generally oversee work in a broad geographic area. They appoint *District Superintendents* to assist with the work in each district. *Pastors* are appointed by the Bishop to preach in each church for a one-year appointment, which may be renewed. In addition to the above offices, there also are elders, deacons and deaconesses, preachers and supply preachers. The *Methodist Discipline*, in paragraphs 251-440, outlines the specific duties and responsibilities of each of these conferences and offices. No attempt is made to give any scriptural authority for this organiza-

tional structure and even for the offices of elders and deacons, the scripture qualifications and duties are not mentioned.

3. Membership in the Methodist Church may be achieved in one of several ways. Children who have been baptized in infancy are to be enrolled in a special class at about age ten and, upon "evidence of understanding their Christian privileges and obligations and of their Christian faith and purpose, they may be admitted into Full Membership in the Church..." (*Discipline*, pgf. 143). Those who present themselves for membership in the Methodist Church shall be instructed "in the principles of the Christian life, in the baptismal and membership vows, and in the rules and regulations of the Methodist Church." When the Pastor is satisfied that the person is willing to accept the above items, he shall present the candidate to the congregation, baptize him, carry out the ritual of entering into a covenant with the membership, then the Pastor shall receive the candidate into the church membership (*Discipline*, pgf. 133).

    "Members in good standing in any evangelical church who desire to unite with us may be received into membership upon giving satisfactory evidence of their willingness to support The Methodist Church and to keep its rules and regulations..." (*Discipline*, pgf. 135).

4. The *name* of the Methodist Church arose from a society of young men which formed at Oxford University in 1727. This group, which eventually included John and Charles Wesley, George Whitefield, and others, met each evening for three hours for study, meditation, and visits to the poor and needy. Their *systematic methods* of carrying out study, meditation, and work led some to call them "Methodists." They accepted the name and it has stayed with them.

D. Presbyterian Church

1. As with Baptists and Methodists, Presbyterians regard themselves as *one among the Protestant denominations*. Since they believe that one is saved through faith only, they regard one as saved before he has

a relationship with any denomination. "The invisible church" is composed of "all true believers of all time" while the "visible church" consists of "all those throughout the world who profess the true religion, together with their children" (Miller, p. 66-67). "Presbyterians cooperate with other denominations in work, at home, and abroad. While loyal to their own standards and convictions, they reach out a hand of fellowship to all evangelical denominations and they seek also the friendship of all communions, even those in which there may be serious differences in both doctrine and polity. They pray earnestly, as the great Head of the church prayed, 'that they may all be one'" (Miller, p. 51).

2. Each *local church* among Presbyterians is part of a representative body called a *"presbytery"* composed of the minister and an elder from each of the churches. The presbyteries of an area are combined in a *"synod,"* composed of representatives from the presbyteries. "The highest court is the General Assembly, which includes all the elected by their respective presbyteries" (Miller, p. 78). Each local church has *bishops or pastors.* "Pastors are called by different names in Scripture because of their varied duties"—bishops, pastors, ministers, presbyters or elders, angels or messengers, ambassadors, stewards. "Ruling elders are representatives of the people and chosen by them for the purpose of exercising government and discipline in conjunction with the pastors or ministers. They are distinguished from the minister by the fact that they do not labor in 'the word and doctrine'" "The office of deacon is based upon Acts 6:1-6, where is described the appointment of persons, presumably deacons, to care for the poor and they may be made responsible for the management of the temporal affairs of the church" (Miller, pp. 76-77).

3. "Provision is made for the reception of *new members* in the church in connection with the Communion. Baptized children are expected in due time to confess their faith in Christ for themselves and to be admitted to the Communion. They are examined by the session and received, and then in the presence of the congregation make their public profession of faith. They thus become commu-

nicant members of the church" (Miller, p. 94). Adults from other denominations are accepted upon a statement that they wish to be associated with the Presbyterians.

4. "Presbyterians get their name from their form of government. They are ruled by elders, the Greek name for which is *presbuteroi*" (Miller, p. 73). Presbyterian, then, signifies that the church follows a "presbyterian" form of government which, as explained above, includes presbyters or overseers in each congregation.

E. Disciples of Christ

1. When the Restoration Movement began, it sought to go back behind denominational structures and "reestablish" the church as it was in the beginning before denominations existed. This undenominational view was held by those associated with the movement until *after* the division into the Christian Church and the church of Christ. The conservatives among the Christian Church still hold this view, but the Disciples of Christ no longer consider that approach valid. Rather, Disciples consider themselves as *one of the denominations*. "The trend of the main body [Disciples] has been in pursuit of the unity of the church and, therefore, has associated itself at every opportunity with interdenominational action and with the ecumenical movement" (Adams, p. 63). "Recent experience in ecumenical conferences, added to that of many Christians under other conditions, demonstrates that there is a fellowship of Spirit that transcends the barriers of creed and custom. These facts and the reality of fellowship make it evident that Christians have not been made Christians by their response to the distinctive beliefs and practices that separate them into denominational churches. Rather, they have been made children of God by their response in faith to the proclamation of the Gospel of Grace, that which is common to all churches" (Adams, p. 73).

2. "By its very nature, a congregationally-governed church, like the Disciples of Christ, does not have and cannot have a strong central organization." The International Convention of Christian Churches (Disciples of Christ) came into being in 1917. Its con-

stitution indicates that the *autonomy of local churches is affirmed* but that there would be certain advantages in having a headquarters (in Indianapolis), coordination of commissions and committees, an annual Convention Assembly, and compilation of a yearbook. There are state conventions which appoint delegates to the Committee on Recommendations but any member is allowed to come to the General Assembly and to vote. The largest agency reporting to the International Convention is the United Christian Missionary Society which administers mission efforts at home and abroad. In addition to state secretaries, there are city secretaries in many of the larger cities who coordinate work among Disciples churches in a metropolitan area (Adams, pp. 74-86).

"The organization of a local Disciple church follows long-established precedents. The official board of a local church is made up of elders, deacons and increasingly, deaconesses. The elders are supposed to be leaders in and guardians over spiritual matters. However, most Disciples ministers, and congregations as well, will confess readily that it is not easy in a Disciple church—nor perhaps in any other church—to distinguish between the things that are essentially spiritual and those that are mundane. Therefore, in most Disciple churches, the elders do not meet separately unless the minister calls them together to help him face a crisis either in his own relations with the church, or in some family in the church, or with the conduct of some officer or member of the church. In most Disciple churches, elders assist the minister at the Communion Table; this is about their only distinguishing service." "But the final authority in every Disciple church is the congregation. The Board of Trustees, elected by the congregation, refers its most important decisions as recommendations to the congregation" (Adams, pp. 87-88).

3. In the early days of the Restoration Movement, baptism for the remission of sins was regarded as essential for all and those who had thus been added to Christ were considered to be members of the church. This view is still held by many in the conservative wing of the Christian Church. Disciples of Christ, however, would gen-

erally practice *"open membership"* by which is meant "the practice of receiving unimmersed Christians from other denominations into full membership of a Disciples of Christ church" (Adams, pp. 46-47). Those who present themselves to become members without having had a previous affiliation, would generally be asked to submit to "believers baptism."

4. As the Restoration Movement sought for a *name* by which it could be designated, several were suggested. Campbell preferred "Disciples of Christ," Stone preferred "Christian Church," and others "church of Christ." All of these terms have been used from time to time among various groups. Today, however, "church of Christ" usually refers to those who work to adhere most closely to the Scriptures, who do not use instrumental music, and who oppose the missionary society. "Christian Church" often identifies those who use the instrument in worship and differ from "churches of Christ" in some other respects but who are still basically conservative. The term "Disciples of Christ" generally applies to those who have a more liberal view and who consider themselves to be members of a denomination.

F. Latter Day Saints

1. Mormons do *not* hold a *denominational* view of the church. Rather, they believe that the church had fallen into an apostate condition and that Joseph Smith, through his direct revelations from God, restored the one true church. Joseph Smith himself was once asked, "Will everybody be damned but Mormons?" His answer was, "Yes, and a great portion of them unless they repent, and work righteousness" (*Teachings of the Prophet Joseph Smith*, p. 119, quoted in Hoekema, p. 63).

2. In *Doctrine and Covenants*, Section 107, Joseph Smith claims to have had a revelation on March 28, 1835, which outlines the *organization* of the Mormon Church. The highest office is that of the *First President*, composed of the President of the Church and two Counselors to the President. Next in authority is the *Council of Twelve Apostles*. In addition to these, there is a *Council of Seventy*.

There are *two priesthoods* in Mormonism: the greater being called after *Melchizedek* and the lesser after *Aaron*. Joseph Smith claimed both. Every male in the Mormon Church may belong to one or the other with 12 years being the minimum age for the Aaronic and 18 the minimum age of the Melchizedek. *Elders* come from the Melchizedek Priesthood while *bishops* come from the Aaronic. "The Mormon Church administration is divided into territories made up of 'wards' and 'stakes,' the former consisting of from five hundred to a thousand people. Each ward is composed of districts known as 'blocks' presided over by a bishop with two teachers and assistants. The wards are all consolidated into stakes, supervised by a president and two counselors, aided in turn by twelve men known as 'The Stake High Council'" (Martin, p. 149; see also Hoekema, p. 17).

3. According to *Doctrine and Covenants*, 20:71—"No one can be received into the church of Christ unless he has arrived unto the years of accountability before God, and is capable of repentance." Baptism is then administered by immersion. Following this, the person is regarded as a member of the church.

4. *Doctrine and Covenants* 115:4 says, "For thus shall my church be called in the last days, even The Church of Jesus Christ of Latter Day Saints." Because the foundation teaching of this church is in *The Book of Mormon*, which Joseph Smith claimed to have translated from Reformed Egyptian, this group is often called the Mormon Church. "Latter Day Saints" is usually preferred although writers in the church itself use both terms.

G. Jehovah's Witnesses

1. Jehovah's Witnesses do *not* accept the *denominational* view of the church. They regard themselves as God's only true people, the Catholic Church as the apostate church, and denominations as false teachers. "Who, then are the ones who form the body of true worshippers today? On the basis of the evidence, which is known or available to persons in all parts of the earth, we do not hesitate to say that they are the Christian witnesses of Jehovah. For you to

share that conviction you need to get well acquainted with them. The best way is to attend their meetings at Kingdom Hall of Jehovah's Witnesses. In this way you can observe for yourself how the organization functions and the way in which those associated with it apply God's Word in their own lives" (*The Truth*, p. 130). "Along with the doctrines of the 'Trinity,' the immortality of the human soul and a hellfire torment, any other teaching or practice that goes contrary to God's inspired Word marks a religion as false and labels it as part of Babylon the Great" (*The Truth*, p. 134).

2. *Headquarters* of the Jehovah's Witness organization is in Brooklyn where the Watchtower Society operates. "Below the central controlling powers are the so-called 'regional servants,' of which there are six in the United States. These supervise the work done in their areas, and report to the Board of Directors. Under these are the 'zone servants,' which number 153 in the United States. These must work with the congregations in their zones and conduct occasional 'zone assemblies' at which the constituent groups meet together. The local groups, which are never larger than two hundred, are called 'companies' or 'congregations,' and the person in charge of each congregation is called a 'company servant'" (Hoekema, p. 326). Jehovah's Witnesses are divided into two groups: (1) the *anointed class* is the 144,000 who will go to heaven and are considered the *only* members of the true church since they have been baptized by the Holy Spirit as well as in water; (2) the *other sheep* who have been baptized in water but will have their reward, not in heaven, but by being raised from the dead to live on the Paradise of the earth (Hoekema, pp. 287-291).

3. *Membership* in the Jehovah's Witnesses comes "when love for God moves you so that you want to do His will, then it is proper that you go to Him in prayer through Jesus Christ and express your desire to be one of His servants" (*Truth*, p. 182). Then, one should be baptized by immersion.

4. The members of the Watchtower Society, in 1931, chose the *name* "Jehovah's Witnesses" from Isaiah 43:10, "Ye are my witnesses, saith Jehovah, and my servant whom I have chosen." They regard

this name as appropriate for they consider themselves the witnesses of God trying to prepare the world for the end of time which will come soon.

H. Seventh-day Adventists

1. There is some controversy among religious writers as to whether Seventh-day Adventists should be considered a *cult* or a *denomination*. The *cult* designation would place it, in their view, with Mormons, Jehovah's Witnesses, and others who are considered outside the general mold of basic Christian views and who, at the same time, treat those who disagree with their teaching with little favor. When these writers list a group as a *denomination*, they are saying that, while the group may have particular beliefs which are outside of the common ones among denominations, they agree in essentials and are accepted by the denominational world.

   Much of the reason for this uncertainty is because the Adventists, themselves, are somewhat ambiguous on the status of those who do not agree with them. Ellen G. White, for example, says that "No one has yet received the mark of the beast. The testing time has not yet come. There are true Christians in every church, not excepting the Roman Catholic communion. None are condemned until they have had the light and seen the obligation of the fourth commandment. But *when the decree shall go forth enforcing the counterfeit sabbath,* and the loud cry of the third angel shall warn men against the worship of the beast and his image, the line will be clearly drawn between the false and the true. *Then those who still continue in transgression will receive the mark of the beast*" (Quoted in Martin, pp. 174-175). This was spoken in 1899 but it does not say when this decree is going forth. Adventists call themselves the "remnant church" but say that there are people in every denomination who remain faithful to the Scriptures" (*Questions on Doctrine*, p. 186).

   The Adventists appear to be in a dilemma on this point. They want to give great emphasis to the teaching about the Sabbath and yet do not want to be placed in the position of saying that those who do not observe the Sabbath Day will, for this reason alone, be lost.

2. The Seventh-day Adventist Church is *administered* through the *executive committee* of their General Conference, chosen by delegates to the General Conference. Under this conference are 12 "division" organizations, working in different continents, 76 "union conferences" and 371 "local conferences." Each local unit is largely autonomous with a congregation electing its own lay elders, deacons, and other officers (Mead, p. 20).

3. Adventists believe that *salvation* is through faith in Christ and repentance. Before one can be admitted to membership in the Seventh-day Adventist Church, however, he must undergo instruction and be baptized. Before baptism, he must give his agreement to keep the teaching of the Church on the sabbath; to give a tithe; and to reject alcoholic beverages, tobacco in all forms, and refuse such foods as coffee, tea, pork, ham, shrimp, lobster, and clams (Hoekema, p. 132-133).

4. The *name* Seventh-day Adventist was adopted as the official name for this religious body in 1860. It expresses two of the most prominent views of the group—keeping the sabbath and expecting the Lord's return or advent to be soon.

I. Assemblies of God

1. The Assemblies of God generally consider themselves a Protestant denomination and have the denominational view of the church. One is saved through faith and then should join the church as a public expression of his salvation (Riggs, p. 141). Their "Statement" calls the "Assemblies of God" a "part of the church" (p. 10).

2. Each *local church* has a measure of independence under its own *pastor* who is the head of the local church. Deacons are appointed to help the pastor, especially with material matters. There are 54 districts, generally following state lines with a district officer who assists churches in his area. A *General Council* is made up of all ordained ministers and a delegate from each local church. This

Council elects all general officers, sets the doctrinal standards, and lays plans for expansion of the church (see Mead, p. 33, and Riggs, p. 119).

3. A new convert should *join a church* so that he may have a better opportunity for service, have the fellowship of other Christians, and have opportunities for worship with others. He should also be baptized as a means of publicly expressing his faith (Riggs, p. 142).

4. The *name* Assembly of God is taken from the fact that the word "church" in the New Testament may be translated "assembly."

J. Church of the Nazarene

1. Nazarenes take the denominational view that all who are saved are members of the "Church of God" and that they then should become associated with a particular church (*Manual*, p. 34-35).

2. The Church of the Nazarene is governed by a General Assembly, District Assemblies, General Superintendents, and District Superintendents. Each congregation has a pastor, sometimes called an elder, who preaches, receives persons for membership, administers sacraments, appoints teachers in Sunday school. Working with him are other local officers such as stewards, deaconesses, trustees, and local church school board (*Manual*, p. 55-94).

3. Those who would join the Nazarenes must first be regenerated, must show a godly walk, and must state their agreement with the fundamental teachings of the Church of the Nazarene. The godly walk includes avoiding the following: taking the name of God in vain, profaning the Lord's Day, drinking intoxicants, taking pride in dress, quarreling, dishonesty, and entertainments such as the theatre, ballroom, or circus (*Manual*, pp. 34-39).

4. The religious body today known as the Church of the Nazarene is the result of the joining of several groups which had names such as Holiness Church, Pentecostal Church, etc. In 1919, the General Assembly adopted the name Church of the Nazarene (*Manual*, pp. 15-23).

Teaching of the Scriptures on Denominationalism, Church Membership, Organization of the Church, Priesthood, and Name

1. The denominational view of the church is that all who have "accepted Christ" or "been born again" *have been saved* and are, therefore, *a part of the church universal.* They may then choose to *join* some denomination or church which believes and practices as they may think best, but since they were *saved before* joining any church, such action has nothing to do with their salvation. This view may be pictured as shown below:

SAVED or CHURCH UNIVERSAL

faith only

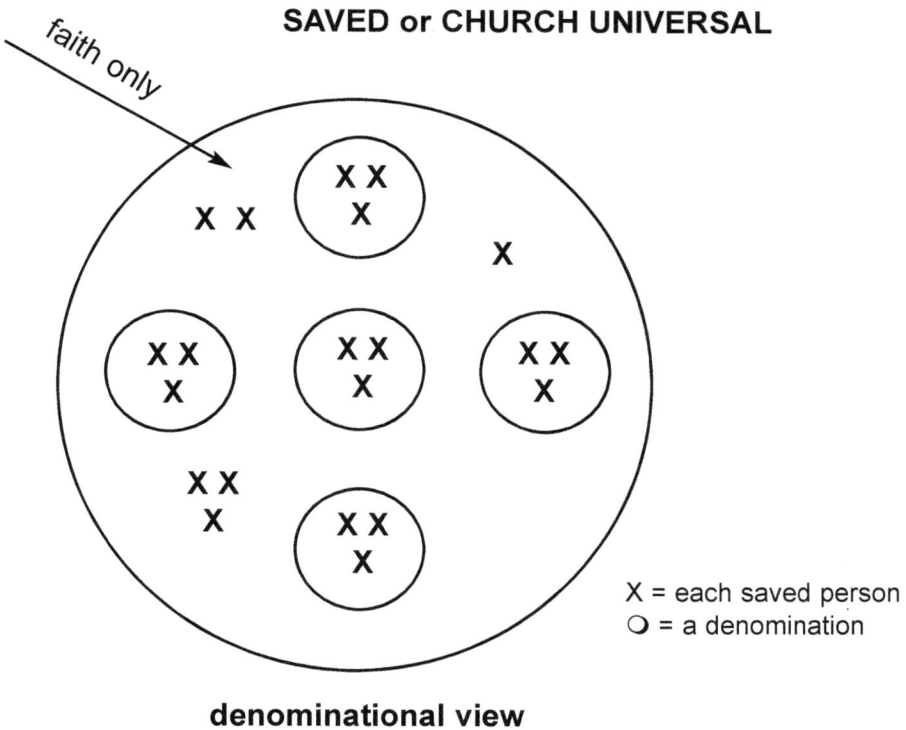

X = each saved person
O = a denomination

denominational view

Contrasting with this is the scriptural view. One is saved through the process of the new birth which involves faith, repentance, and baptism and, at that point, *after baptism*, one is "added" to the saved (Acts 2:47), placed "into Christ" (Galatians 3:27), starts the "new life" (Romans 6:4), is "saved" (Mark 16:16), has his sins "forgiven" (Acts 2:38), has his sins "washed away" (Acts 22:16), and is put "into" the one body (I Corinthians 12:12, 13). Once in this body of the saved, there should be *no* additional joining of subgroups that divide believers. Paul was very explicit about such actions in I Corinthians 1:10, Galatians 5:19-21, and Jesus prayed that His followers might all be one (John 17:17). All the illustrations of the church suggest its oneness: kingdom, body, bride, vine, family. So, we might diagram the biblical view as follows:

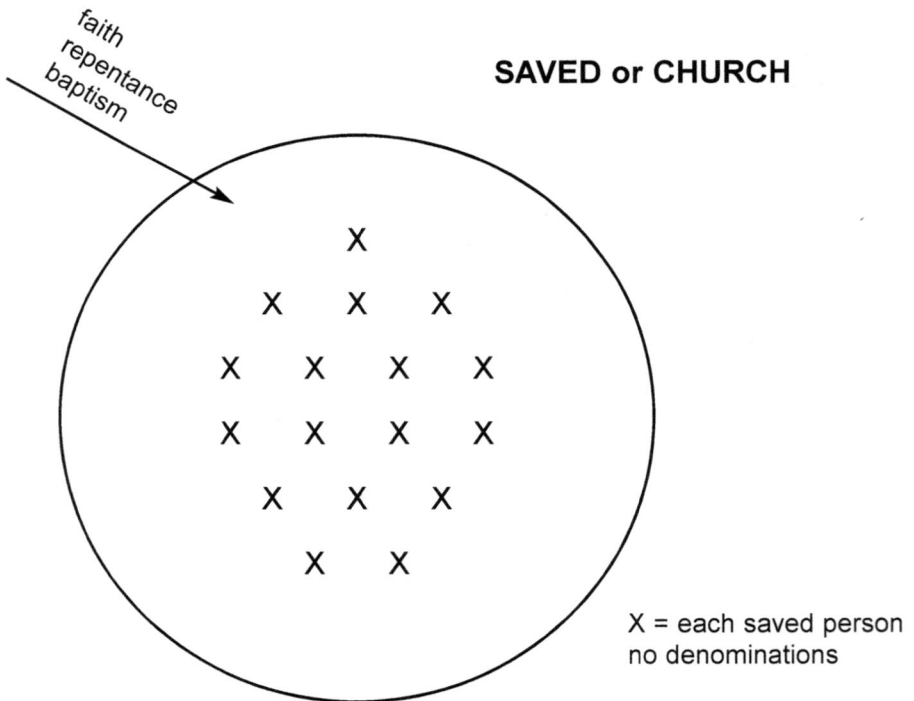

faith
repentance
baptism

SAVED or CHURCH

X
X X X
X X X X
X X X X
X X X
X X

X = each saved person
no denominations

2. *Membership in the church* or body of Christ is not, therefore, a matter of joining something *after* one is saved. *The very process of being saved is the same process by which one becomes a member of the body.* It is not scriptural to speak of "joining the church" for it is God who "adds" when one is saved. One may, however, "join himself" to a

local congregation of the church to place himself in fellowship with other Christians in his locality (Acts 9:26).

The Restoration Movement, which began about 1750 to 1800 within various denominations, was an effort to get *outside* the denominational structures which prevented one from following the Bible *only* and getting back to "original ground." As the diagram below indicates, there was a departure from the "faith once for all delivered to the saints" (Jude 3) even as Paul had predicted (I Timothy 4:1-4; II Timothy 4:1-4; Acts 20:29-30). He had particularly warned that there was *no other gospel* and any who preached contrary to what he had received directly from God was to be accursed (Galatians 1:7-12). As these departures came and were followed by the majority of professing Christians, the Catholic Church had its origin. Eventually, as shown on the chart, reformers like Luther and Calvin tried to move back down the line to undo some of the departures, but they were unable to do that within the structure of the Catholic Church. They moved outside, therefore, establishing "protesting" or Protestant groups. Eventually, these became fixed in certain doctrines and many new groups were established, each attempting to move toward the Scriptures in some particular point. By 1800, it was evident to many, however, that this approach would never result in the unity of believers or in returning to the "apostles' doctrine" which one could be certain was the will of God. So, from many different points, they said, let's take the Bible as a blueprint or "seed" and start over, doing only what the Scriptures authorize. After following this procedure for a time, they learned of others who had done the same thing and who had come to similar conclusions. This process is still going on as new groups from over the world learn of each other.

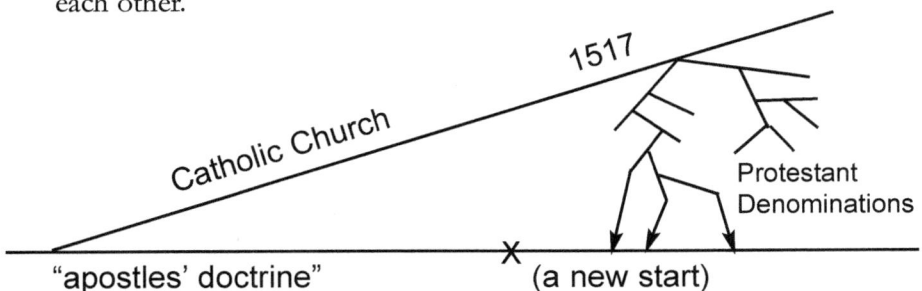

"apostles' doctrine"   X (a new start)

3. The *organization* of the church in the New Testament was always *congregational*, with each local body directing its own affairs through its own elders, bishops, or pastors. These three words all refer to the same persons and these officers are always spoken of in the plural, indicating that a *group* of men, not *one*, was responsible for the local work. Their qualifications are clearly stipulated in Titus 1 and I Timothy 3 and their work is mentioned in various places such as Acts 20:28-31; I Peter 5:1-4; I Timothy 3:1-7, Titus 1:5-9; I Timothy 5:17-19. In addition to elders or bishops or pastors, each local congregation also had *deacons* as outlined in I Timothy 3:8-13. The church of the first century also had apostles, prophets, evangelists, and teachers (Ephesians 4:11). "Apostles" were appointed as witnesses of Christ's resurrection and to carry out certain work as the church began. No one today could qualify as an apostle (Acts 1:21, 22). Prophets and others with spiritual gifts were also for revealing of the Word and its confirmation. These gifts were intended only for the childhood of the church (I Corinthians 13:8-13). This leaves "evangelists" or "preachers" and "teachers" along with "elders" and "deacons" for the work of the church today.

Since the church had no organization above that of the *local congregation* and each of these local units was autonomous, there should be no superstructure for the church today. The situation in Acts 15 is sometimes cited as a basis for church assemblies or conferences, but such is a misunderstanding of what happened. This meeting was not called for a vote of men on what doctrines the church should follow. Rather, apostles, men guided by the Holy Spirit, demonstrated they had all received the same revelation. Since some were saying that Paul, an apostle, was preaching a different doctrine about the Law of Moses than the apostles in Jerusalem were, this occasion was a demonstration they all stood together. A careful reading of the passage will show there was no voting, no delegates, and no new creeds written. The communication that followed the discussions confirmed that Paul's teaching was in harmony with that of other apostles.

4. The New Testament Church had *no special priesthood* but all members were part of the holy priesthood and thus each could come equally before God through Jesus Christ (1 Peter 2:5, 9; Revelation 1:6; Hebrews 4:14-16). The Mormon doctrine that persons today can be in the Aaronic and Melchizedek priesthoods is not in harmony with the teaching of the book of Hebrews. The Aaronic priesthood was established as a part of the Law of Moses, was for the Israelites, and, to be a member of this priesthood, one had to be of a particular family within the Tribe of Levi. Since Christ was of the Tribe of Judah, even He could not be of the Aaronic priesthood. Rather, He was a priest after the order of Melchizedek because He did not receive the priesthood through family ties. Hebrews 7:11-28 makes it clear that the Aaronic priesthood has been changed an in its place comes Christ, after the order of Melchizedek. Each Christian is a priest in the sense that Christ has made it possible for each to come before God in prayer directly without the need for an intervening human agency.

5. The name applied to followers of Christ was "Christian" and as a body, they were usually called simply "the church." Often, however, the church was referred to by a designation of ownership such as the "church of God" (1 Corinthians 1:1) or "churches of Christ" (Romans 16:16). It is good to realize that there was no formal title which was always used in referring to Christ's body and that any of the ways in which the Scriptures refer to these disciples would be appropriate. If we are going to follow the principle of "speaking where the Bible speaks," however, we should use only those names which the Bible uses in speaking of Christ's body. Since there are so many different religious groups today with similar names, it appears wise to use one of these scriptural designations consistently. We should not, however, do this to the exclusion of other Scripture terms lest we distort the teaching of the Scripture on this matter. Those using names *not* found in the Scripture are, of course, departing from the New Testament pattern at least to that extent.

VI. Worship

A. Roman Catholic

Worship in the Catholic Church usually is built around observance of the *mass*. Daily mass is observed and is regarded as a *perpetual sacrifice of Christ's blood*. Gibbons explains it this way: "The sacrifice of the Mass is the consecration of the bread and wine into the body and blood of Christ, and the oblation of this body and blood to God, by the ministry of the Priest, for a perpetual memorial of Christ's sacrifice on the cross. The Sacrifice of the Mass is identical with that of the cross, both having the same victim and High Priest—Jesus Christ. The only difference consists in the manner of the oblation. Christ was offered up on the cross in a bloody manner, and in the Mass He is offered up in an unbloody manner. On the cross He purchased our ransom, and in the Eucharistic Sacrifice the price of that ransom is applied to our souls. Hence, all the efficacy of the Mass is derived from the sacrifice of Calvary" (Gibbons, pp. 254-255).

To Catholics, then, the *bread* becomes the *actual body* of Christ and the *wine* His *actual blood*. This is called "The Real Presence" or "transubstantiation" and this has been one of the controversial points between Catholics and Protestants. Speaking of the bread and fruit of the vine, Jesus said, "This is my body and this is my blood." Catholics take this as literally and not figuratively true. In this way, they claim, the actual sacrifice of Christ's body and blood are repeated wherever the mass is conducted. (See Gibbons, Chapters XXI, XXII, and XXIII for more details.)

Catholics, since about the fifteenth century, have offered *only the bread* to the communicant with the *priest* partaking of the wine. It is their view that this is simpler, that it reduces the problem of providing "consecrated wine" for large numbers, that it avoids the possibility of spilling the wine and thus profaning it, and that it is sufficient to take either the bread or the wine without both. Of late, they have begun, to some extent, to restore the practice of allowing members to partake of both the bread and the cup.

Worship among Catholics is *highly ritualistic and ceremonial.* There are many symbols, spoken formulae, vestments for the priests, burning of incense, etc. Since about the fifteenth century, *instrumental music,* primarily the organ, has been used.

Individual worship is also encouraged and if one enters a Catholic cathedral, he will often see someone *burning a candle,* reciting prayers with a *rosary,* or in some other type of individual worship.

B. Baptists

In their worship, Baptists sing, with the accompaniment of instruments; pray; study the Bible; give offerings; and partake of the Lord's Supper. They do not practice rituals and ceremonies similar to those of the Catholic Church. They have choirs and soloists but also engage in congregational singing.

Their position on the Lord's Supper is clearly stated by Hobbs:

> There are four basic historic views relative to this ordinance. The Roman Catholic position is that of transubstantiation or "substance across." It holds that in the Mass the bread and the wine become the body and blood of Jesus. (Note: the New Testament does not say "wine" but "fruit of the vine.") Lutherans believe in consubstantiation. This view holds that the body and blood of Jesus are present within the elements of the Lord's Supper. Others hold to the view that grace is present with the elements, or that the partaker receives grace thereby which is not available otherwise. Baptists believe that the Lord's Supper is symbolic. The bread and fruit of the vine are but symbols of the broken body and spilled blood of Jesus. (Hobbs, p. 84)

Additional information on the Baptist view of the Lord's Supper is found in the *Church Member's Handbook* by Odle:

> Christian denominations generally agree that only the baptized should take the Supper. Baptists do not accept anything as baptism

except immersion on profession of faith. Most Southern Baptists also believe that this must be administered by a Baptist church. Churches that do not invite others to partake of the Supper are thus being consistent with their convictions about baptism.

Is open communion possible? No! Paul's statement in I Corinthians 11:18-20 shows that open communion is impossible! "For first of all, when ye come together in the church, I hear that there be divisions among you; and I partly believe it. For there must be also heresies among you, that they which are approved may be made manifest among you. When ye come together therefore into one place, this is not to eat the Lord's Supper."

Suppose that four denominations are gathered together in "open communion." There are divisions and heresies there, for they certainly do not believe and teach the same doctrines. Paul says that such a group cannot eat the "Lord's Supper," for it will not be the "Lord's Supper." Open communion is impossible!

How often should the Lord's Supper be observed? There is no command as to this. The Scriptures simply say "as often as ye eat." Some churches observe it yearly, some quarterly, others more often. (Odle, pp. 23-24)

C. Methodists

The *Methodist Discipline* suggests four basic *orders of worship* which include the following parts of the worship in different orders: The Prelude, The Call to Worship, A Hymn, The Prayer of Confession, The Silent Meditation, The Words of Assurance, The Lord's Prayer, The Anthem or Chant, The Responsive Reading, The Gloria Patri, The Affirmation of Faith, The Lesson From the Holy Scriptures, The Pastoral Prayer, The Offertory, A Hymn, The Sermon, The Prayer, The Invitation to Christian Discipleship, The Benediction, The Silent Prayer, The Postlude. Variations are suggested for those services which are to include an observance of the communion. As can be seen from the above, the Methodist Church includes more ritual and *ceremony* than, for example, the Baptist Church. They likewise use *instruments* of music, choirs, and soloists in their services. Methodists invite "all followers of Christ who desire to partake with us of the symbols of the body and blood of our Lord" (Selecman, p. 38). The *Methodist Discipline* makes the following statement regarding the Lord's Supper which they take at least once a quarter but some as often as once a week:

> The Supper of the Lord is not only a sign of the love that Christians ought to have among themselves one to another, but rather is a Sacrament of our redemption by Christ's death; insomuch that, to such as rightly, worthily, and with faith receive the same, the bread which we break is a partaking of the body of Christ; and likewise the cup of blessing is a partaking of the blood of Christ.

> Transubstantiation, or the change of the substance of bread and wine in the Supper of our Lord, cannot be proved by the Holy Spirit, but is repugnant to the plain words of Scripture, overthroweth the nature of a Sacrament, and hath given occasion to many superstitions...

> The Cup of the Lord is not to be denied to the Lay People; for both the parts of the Lord's Supper, by Christ's ordinance and commandment, ought to be administered to all Christians alike.

> The offering of Christ, once made, is that perfect redemption, propitiation, and satisfaction for all the sins of the whole world, both original and actual; that there is none other satisfaction for sin but that alone. Wherefore the sacrifice of masses, in the which it is commonly said that the priest doth offer Christ for the quick and the dead, to have remission of pain or guilt, is a blasphemous fable and dangerous deceit. (*Discipline*, pp. 78-80)

Methodists *do not require tithing* but their plan for financing church operations includes informing the membership of the needs, asking for systematic contributions, and the use of envelopes. "Quarterly or semi-annual statements should be issued and arrears collected so far as possible," and every member is sought as a "recorded contributor" (*Discipline*, p. 815).

Women are allowed to take a leading part in the worship as readers or in other capacities at some Methodist Churches.

D. Presbyterians

The Presbyterians have a *Book of Common Worship* which sets forth generally the plan of worship to be followed. It includes praise in song, prayers, sermon, offering, and communion. The use of *instruments* of music is allowed and choirs and soloists are permitted.

The offering is to be systematic and in proportion to the individual's prosperity." The Lord's Supper, or the Communion, is to be celebrated as often as the minister and session think wise, so as not to have it so frequently that it loses its significance through familiarity, and yet often enough to provide the inspiration and spiritual growth which Christians need. (This observance is usually quarterly.) The minister explains the meaning of the Lord's Supper as instituted by Christ, reads the words of institution, invites those who should partake of the bread and the cup, sets the elements apart by prayer, and the bread and cup are distributed by the elders. A brief meditation usually precedes the administration of the sacrament, and is followed by a prayer of thanksgiving, penitence, and dedication. A collection for the poor is associated with the observance of the Lord's Supper" (Miller, p. 94).

E. Disciples of Christ

Worship among Disciples is *less formal* and ceremonial than among Methodists and Presbyterians and usually some variety in order is practiced. Each local congregation determines the order of worship. *Instruments* of music are allowed with the singing, and prayer, giving, and the Lord's Supper are part of the service. The Communion is observed *each Sunday* and it is regarded as symbolic of the body and blood of Christ. The "elaborate mystery of the Mass of the Roman Catholic Church" is rejected (Adams, pp. 54-55). "All Christians" are invited to share in the communion (Adams, p. 57).

F. Latter Day Saints

Mormons meet each Sunday for worship including *weekly observance of the Lord's Supper.* According to a revelation to Joseph Smith in August of 1830 as he was on the way to purchase wine for the communion, he was told "it mattereth not what ye shall eat or what ye shall drink when ye partake of the sacrament, if it so be that he do it with an eye single to my glory—remembering unto the Father my body which was laid down for you, and my blood which was shed, for the remission of your sins" (*Doctrine and Covenants*, 27:2). *Light bread and water* are now commonly used instead of the unleavened bread and grape juice.

Tithing is taught in *Doctrine and Covenants*, Section 119.

Talmadge in *Articles of Faith*, p. 175, states that the Lord's Supper is not a means for securing the remission of sins but is a testimony of our faithfulness and determination and a means for receiving "a continuing endowment of the Holy Spirit."

The well-known Mormon Tabernacle Choir illustrates the Mormon view of the use of choirs and *instruments* of music in worship.

G. Jehovah's Witnesses

Jehovah's Witnesses meet weekly at their local Kingdom Hall for Bible study, singing, and praying. They do not take up collections at such meetings, and those not members are invited (*Truth*, p. 138). Women are allowed to speak: "But regardless of popular custom, if a woman today should arise in a congregation and pray or prophesy to the believing men and women present, she should veil her head or have a 'sign of authority upon her head because of the angels'" (*Everlasting Life*, p. 162). The *oppose celebrating Christmas and Easter* as special occasions because these were not initiated by Christ or observed by early Christians but come from pagan sources (*Truth*, p. 147). They also are opposed to all images and pictures or crosses in religious services (*Truth*, pp. 140-147).

They observe the Lord's Supper *once a year*, after sundown on the exact day of the year Christ died. Unleavened bread and fermented wine are used to symbolize Christ's body and blood. They reject the doctrine of transubstantiation. They teach that the communion is intended to be celebrated only by those who are included in the 144,000 or anointed class. Those among the "other sheep" are to attended the annual Memorial Service but are not to partake. (See Hoekema, pp. 292-293.)

H. Seventh-day Adventists

Worship services among the Seventh-day Adventists, of course, are held on the *Sabbath* which begins Friday at sundown and lasts until Saturday at sundown. They follow a rather *set order* of prayers, songs, collection, and sermon. Instrumental music is used and some groups have choirs.

They usually observe the *Lord's Supper* once a quarter and always precede this observance with footwashing which they consider also as a symbolic ceremony.

In their doctrine, *baptism* is symbolic of the washing from sins prior to becoming a Christian while *footwashing* is symbolic of the regular washing of sins after one is a Christian. Men and women are separated for the footwashing. (See Hoekema, p. 134 and Branson, pp. 183-184.)

Tithing is required and each local group sends its tithes to their national headquarters which, in turn, pays all ministers the same salary regardless of the size of the group served. Some groups decide to contribute above the tithe for local use.

I. Assemblies of God

The Assemblies of God worship each Sunday with praying, singing, teaching, and contribution. They ask members to *tithe* and cite the following passages: Malachi 3:10; I Corinthians 16:1, 2; II Corinthians 8:1-4 (Riggs, pp. 142-143). They use *instrumental music* with their singing. The *Lord's Supper* is recognized as symbolic of Christ's body and blood and the teaching of transubstantiation is rejected. It is usually observed *once a month* and also on special occasions such as Thanksgiving. The communion is related to divine healing for they say "By faith as we partake of these emblems we can appropriate the quickening life of Christ for our healing. Isaiah 53:5; I Peter 2:24; Matthew 8:17; I Corinthians 11:27-30; John 6:51, 55, 56" (Riggs, pp. 118-119). *Women* are allowed to preach.

J. Church of the Nazarene

The Nazarenes have singing, prayer, and preaching in their services. There is, however, a *standard ritual* suggested for observing the Lord's Supper (Manual, p. 311). The minister is to invite "all those who have with true repentance forsaken their sins, and have believed in Christ unto salvation" to draw near and take the emblems. Nazarenes use *instrumental music* and have choirs and soloists. *Women* are allowed to preach.

Teaching of the Scripture on Worship

If we follow the principle of doing only what the Scriptures tell us to do in worship, then we will worship as Christians in the New Testament did: praying together (Acts 12:5, 12); singing together (Colossians 3:16; Galatians 5:19); hearing a preacher (Acts 20:7) or reading from the Scriptures (Colossians 4:16); giving of our money to support the work (I Corinthians 16:12); and partaking of the Lord's Supper, often called "breaking bread" (Acts 20:7). When we are doing these things in the way the Holy Spirit instructed first-century Christians, we can be sure our worship is acceptable. Serious penalties are suggested in the Scriptures for those who seek to worship God in any way other than what He has instructed (Matthew 15:9; Leviticus 10:1, 2; I Samuel 13:8-15; I Corinthians 11:17-33).

Unfortunately, through the years, many changes have been made in this simple, meaningful worship. Some of these changes mentioned above in the discussion of various religions are listed below with passages that indicate the view of the Scriptures on these points.

1. *The observance of the Lord's Supper.* There is no scriptural basis for suggesting that the partaker of the communion receives some *special blessing* or *forgiveness*. It is never mentioned that this memorial is a reenactment of the sacrifice of Christ and must be repeated daily to keep its power applied to Christians. Rather, Hebrews 7:26-28 makes it clear that, unlike the Old Testament sacrifices which did have to be offered daily, the sacrifice of Christ under the New Covenant was given "once for all." Catholics say that in its "bloody form," once is enough, but it must be repeated daily in its "unbloody form" through the Mass. Of this there is, of course, no mention in the Scriptures.

   Because Catholics teach that one receives forgiveness of sins by participating in the Mass (Smith, p. 912), many Protestant sects also give the communion some special power. The Lord's Supper, rather, is a solemn memorial, done in memory of Christ's death and resurrection, and, as such, does recognize the power of Christ's blood to save from sin; but nowhere do the Scriptures teach that one applies to blood to his sins by taking the Lord's Supper. Initial forgiveness comes at the point one reenacts Christ's death and resurrection in baptism (Romans 6:4) and a continuing cleansing of His blood comes to those who "walk in the light" (I

John 1:7). The communion is an act of worship and, like any worship, must be observed seriously, but *it offers no more special benefits than any other act of worship.*

The doctrine of transubstantiation is also a perversion of original teaching. Christ did say of the bread, "This is my body," and of the fruit of the vine, "This is my blood." These statements, however, may *either* be taken literally or figuratively. Jesus also said He was "water," "a door," "a vine," and other things which must be taken figuratively. What Jesus meant by calling the bread His "body" and the wine His "blood" can be determined three ways. First, in the passage itself, would the apostles have more likely taken the statement literally or figuratively? If He meant it literally, then He was giving His apostles *His real body and blood* while *He was still alive.* Surely, the prohibitions against drinking blood would have come to their mind from Genesis 9:4. With the simple statement and no further explanation, the apostles certainly would not have thought Jesus was speaking of drinking His actual blood or eating His real body. Second, the passage in John 6:48-58 where Jesus refers to eating His flesh and drinking His blood does not refer to eating the Lord's Supper as Catholics suggest. In the entire passage Jesus is making a point about His feeding of the 5,000 (vss. 26, 27) and is trying to tell the Jews that they are mistaking physical food for spiritual. Coming to Him involves "learning" (vss. 44, 45) and "believing" (v. 47). If eating His flesh means taking of the Lord's Supper, then everyone who eats of the bread alone receives eternal life (v. 51). Even Catholics teach that serious sins are not forgiven by the Mass, only lesser ones (Smith, p. 912). If, on the other hand, Christ is here speaking of believing and acting on His words, then this alone does bestow eternal life. When the disciples asked Him to explain, Jesus said it was the *spiritual,* not the fleshly, that profited and then explained that He meant *"the words"* He had spoken were the spirit of life He had spoken of (v. 63). Peter understood Christ to be speaking of this message: "To whom shall we go? Thou hast the words of eternal life" (v. 68). To make eating actual bread and wine to be the means for a great spiritual blessing is exactly the opposite of Jesus' teaching here for His whole point is not to think of physical food but of spiritual food (His words) as the way to eternal life. Third, nowhere else in the Scriptures is the doctrine of transubstantiation suggested and it was not until many centuries later that it came into the common belief of Catholics. In fact, not until the Council of Trent in 1551 was it made an article of faith.

If one seeks to follow the New Testament pattern, he would, of course, *use only unleavened bread and fruit of the vine in the communion.* These were among the very specifically designated items on the table when Jesus ate the Passover meal and it was at such a meal that Christ initiated the Lord's Supper. These elements are specifically mentioned in Matthew 26:26-29; Mark 14:22-24; Luke 22:19, 20; John 13:1-4; I Corinthians 10:16-21; 11:23-29. There is no justification for any substitution.

As to *frequency with which the Lord's Supper was observed* by the early Christians when they were being guided directly by the Holy Spirit, there are several ways to determine the answer. *First,* one may consider that Christians assembled every first day of the week, for in I Corinthians 16:1, 2 Paul uses a Greek phrase, *kata mian,* which may well be translated "very first" to modify "of the week." He told them, then, "every first day of the week," they were to "lay by in store," and most churches today practice weekly giving. From I Corinthians 11:20, however, it is apparent that when the Corinthians had this weekly assembly, it was customary to take the Lord's Supper. Paul criticizes them because their abuses were making this observance impossible to observe properly.

Second, the example of the early church was to take the Lord's Supper each first day of the week. In Acts 20:7, we are told that Paul waited seven days so he could meet with the disciples who were going to meet on the first day of the week to "break bread." This phrase was used to mean the communion as in Acts 2:42 where it is mentioned in a list of items of Christian worship. So the disciples were coming together "on the first day of the week to break bread." The clear suggestion of this passage is that their practice was to break bread *each* first day of the week for if their custom had been on "the first Sunday of the month" or "the last Sunday of the quarter," then the wording would have been in those words. "First day" names the specific part of a period, and "week" names the period.

Third, the testimony of early writers among Christians is clear, also, that the early practice was to take of the communion weekly. "All antiquity concurs in evincing that, for the *three first centuries*, all the churches broke bread once a week. Pliny, in his *Epistles*, Book X; Justin Martyr, in his *Second Apology for the Christians;* and Tertullian, *De Ora.* Page 135; testify that it was the universal practice in all the weekly assemblies of the brethren" (Campbell, *Christianity Restored*, p. 336).

2. There is no suggestion in the New Testament Scriptures that there is any *priesthood* in the church outside of Christ as the high priest (Hebrews 7) and individual Christians as priests (I Peter 2:5, 9; Revelation 1:6). Hebrews 13:10-16 contrasts our individual sacrifices of praise and good works with the sacrifices of the Old Testament and suggests that each Christian offers his own. There is *no indication of ritual or specific ceremonies* in the worship of the early church. By all historical accounts they followed a very simple service of singing, praying, reading and commenting on the Scriptures, giving, and observing the Lord's Supper weekly. Paul specifically forbids the observance of "days, and months, and seasons, and years" as a continuation of the system of Law which has passed away (Galatians 4:10, 11). Every Christian is equally free to come "with boldness unto the throne of grace" (Hebrews 4:16) with Christ as our only mediator (I Timothy 2:5).

3. This same passage which states that there is "one mediator" also *forbids the use of saints or others as mediators* between us and God. To say that praying first to Mary or some other person designated a "saint" is more effective than coming directly through Christ suggests that Christ is less than a perfect mediator. Paul would not allow himself to be worshiped as a god (Acts 14:11-15) nor would Peter allow Cornelius to fall before him (Acts 10:25, 26). Even an

angel would not allow John to fall down before him, but said, "See thou do it not: I am a fellow-servant with thee and with thy brethren the prophets, and with them that keep the words of this book: worship God" (Revelation 22:9). Those who would use images, burn incense and candles, and offer repetitive prayers should first recognize that early Christians were not guided into these practices by the Holy Spirit and then consider that images are forbidden (I Thessalonians 1:9), that the use of repetitious phrases in prayers are condemned (Matthew 6:7, 8), and that carrying Old Testament forms of worship into Christian practice is rejected in Colossians 2:13-23).

4. The question of *instrumental music in Christian worship* has long been a controversial one. If the question is, "What was the practice of Christians in the days when the apostles and others were divinely guided?", then there can be agreement about the answer. Both from the New Testament and from history comes the same answer: the church of the first century used *vocal music only*. If one is seeking to follow the New Testament church as a pattern, then the answer is simple. If one wishes to go to the next step and ask, "But what difference does it make?", then he should consider the many warnings of "not to go beyond the things that are written" (I Corinthians 4:6) and the consequences of presenting to God in worship that which He has not commanded. Singing as a means of Christian worship is mentioned five times, but each time it is spoken of in terms of vocal music only and never of playing an instrument (Acts 16:25; I Corinthians 14:15; Ephesians 5:19; Colossians 3:16; and James 5:13). One can sing and clearly be within the commandment, but not so with playing an instrument.

Those who justify the instrument in worship must do so on one of two grounds but never both: (1) the playing of an instrument is *an act of Christian worship* even as it was for the Jews (Psalm 150:3-5), or (2) that it is *only an insignificant aid* to the singing and is not actually an addition to the New Testament pattern. The first option is clearly unacceptable, for to bring instrumental music into Christian services on the basis of its use in the Old Testament would violate the teaching that the law is no longer binding, and would also open the door for incense, animal sacrifices, and the brazen laver. To justify instruments on the basis of their being "an aid," on the other hand, means taking what was, on its own, an act of worship during the Jewish age, and making it *merely an aid* during the Christian age. Even the question of whether it aids the singing is open to serious question. The best congregational singing is clearly among those who do not use the instrument for those who do use it tend to rely on it too much. Moreover, most of those who use instruments do not limit their being played to times when the singing is being done but use it in many other parts of the worship as well. *No one* can question that it is acceptable to sing without instruments, so *why take the chance?* That singing among Christ's followers was entirely vocal for centuries is clear from history. The addition of instruments came with great controversy in the Catholic Church with some of their most famous theologians such as Thomas Aquinas opposing it. When the Reformation Movement came, many leaders such as John Calvin, John Knox, John Wesley, Charles Spurgeon, Adam Clarke, and many others opposed its use.

5. Many denominations require *tithing* in Christian giving. Does this practice of the Jews apply to Christians? As explained earlier, it cannot be applied to Christians on the basis of its being required under the Law of Moses for that law has passed away and neither Jews nor Gentiles are now under its ordinances. Is tithing taught in the New Testament? No passage on Christian giving even mentions tithing or giving of *any* specified percentage. A Christian, rather, is exhorted to give as he has "prospered" (I Corinthians 16:2), "liberally" (II Corinthians 8:2) to show "proof of love" (II Corinthians 8:24), "bountifully" (II Corinthians 9:6), "cheerfully" (II Corinthians 9:7), and "not grudgingly nor of necessity" (II Corinthians 9:7). All of these Scriptures state that giving is on a "free-will" basis and not by requirement. Hopefully, a Christian will *exceed* the tithing of the Old Testament, but there is no New Testament requirement to tithe.

6. Many denominations, or at least some churches or branches of some denominations, are now *allowing women to preach, pray, and lead other parts in their worship services.* This practice may vary among various groups within denominations, but where it does occur, it is a violation of Paul's clear statement in I Corinthians 14:34, 35 and I Timothy 2:8-15.

VII. Last Things

A. Roman Catholic

Catholics believe that the *soul* of man is spiritual and as such it is eternal. "Death makes no difference to the soul's real status, it becomes neither more spiritual or more imperishable than it is during man's lifetime; it remains what is has always been—an unmixed spiritual substance" (Smith, p. 1112). At death, according to the Catholic Church, a soul may have one of three states: (1) "If it be in a state of perfect charity, will enter into heavenly bliss, without any retardation" and "will not be in a state of unconsciousness, but will be fully aware of its own existence, its election, its final escape from evil," "a state of expectation"; (2) "if the soul of the Christian, though in a state of grace at death, yet be not perfect in charity, then admission to heavenly bliss is retarded; the soul is perfected through a mysterious process called purgatory"; (3) and finally the reprobates who die "in a state of mortal sin" will be "cast into eternal death" (Smith, pp. 1115, 1132). *Purgatory* is that place of departed souls who are "in a state of grace" but who are appointed to "suffer for a time after death on account of their sins; either for venial sins that are not repented nor forgiven before death; or for sins whose guilt was forgiven in this life, but whose due of punishment is to be completed after death" (Smith, pp. 1115, 1141). Gibbons bases his argument for purgatory primarily on a passage in the apocryphal II Maccabees 12:43-46 from which he concludes that praying for forgiveness of sins on behalf of the dead was a practice that was common among Jews of Jesus' day and Jesus never corrected them. He also refers to Matthew 12:32 and I Corinthians 3:13-15.

Catholics teach that there will be four manifestations of God's power when "the day of the Lord" comes: "there will be the destruction of the physical world through fire; there will be the raising up of all the dead; there will be the revelation of all the hidden things of man's conscience and God's providence; and then, ultimately, there will be the separation of the good and the wicked" (Smith, p. 1136). From this passage it is clear that Catholics believe that *when Christ comes*, He will being an end to the present world, not start a 1,000-year kingdom (Smith, p. 1140). They believe that all the dead will be raised at one time, not in a series of separate resurrections of the good and the wicked (Smith, p. 1109). They believe in a last judgment where "all the human beings that ever existed" will be gathered before God where they "will be separated again, and this for all eternity" (Smith, p. 1135). "Eternal punishment is the everlasting separation of God from the sinner, because the sinner continues to reject Him…and can no longer change his mind" (Smith, p. 1177). Heaven, on the other hand, is the great victory where those who have fought the good fight will see God face to face (Smith, p. 1249).

B. Baptists

"At physical death, therefore, all enter Hades and remain in a conscious state. The lost endure punishment; the saved enjoy fellowship with Christ (cf. Luke 16). At the judgment this state of each is fixed eternally. There is no scriptural basis for 'soul sleeping.' 'Hades' is never used in the sense of purgatory. No such idea is taught in the New Testament" (Hobbs, p. 109).

"Those Christians who are alive at Christ's second coming shall be changed immediately (I Corinthians 15:51 ff.). But their translation into heaven will be preceded by the bodily resurrection of those who lie in the cemetery (I Thessalonians 4:15-18). God will bring the souls of the righteous dead with him to be united with their resurrection bodies (I Thessalonians 4:14). All will be caught up to meet the Lord in the air. "And so shall we ever be with the Lord" (I Thessalonians 4:17) (Hobbs, p. 110).

Hobbs continues about the second coming suggesting from Matthew 24 that "men will mistake normal happenings of history as signs of his return. We are not to be deceived thereby. Life will go its normal way, until without warning he will appear (vv. 37-39)." "Since his coming will be outward, visible, and personal (Acts 1:11)," a Christian should live in "constant expectancy (Matthew 24:44)." "At the Lord's return there will be the resurrection of the dead and the transformation of the living (1 Thessalonians 4:13-18). Here Paul is thinking of those who are in Christ" (Hobbs, pp. 111-112).

Hobbs suggests three general views of the millennium. "Postmillennialsim believes that after a thousand years of peace and righteousness, made possible by the gospel, Christ will return with one general resurrection and judgment, followed by the eternal reign of Christ. Premillennialism holds that Christ will return before the thousand years. It sees two resurrections and two or more judgments, followed by Christ's earthly reign. There are varying positions within this group, some of which deal with minute details of events. A-millennialism regards the thousand years as figurative. The word 'a-millennium' means 'no millennium' or that the thousand years are not to be taken literally (cf. II Peter 3:8). To this group the return of Christ will be attended by one general resurrection and judgment which will terminate history and inaugurate Christ's eternal reign. Within this group one position (e.g. Augustine) regards the millennium as the entire Christian era which terminates with Christ's return. Another (e.g. Kliefoth) holds the millennium to be the eternal, heavenly state itself" (Hobbs, pp. 112-113).

Hobbs states that Baptists generally hold to either the premillennial or the a-millennial position, but that "One's position on this has never been a test of faith or fellowship among them" (Hobbs, p. 113).

As Hobbs suggests, Baptists do not all agree on the 1000-year reign. It should be noted, however, that Billy Graham and many other prominent Baptists do hold that Christ will return to start an earthly reign of a thousand years.

C. Methodists

The Methodist Church takes no official position on the millennium but has members who believe in the thousand-year reign and some who do not. The *Discipline* does deny the doctrine of purgatory and Methodists would generally believe in the punishment of the wicked and eternal bliss of the righteous.

D. Presbyterians

"The Confession of Faith also deals with the state of man after death. At death their bodies decay and return to dust, but their souls, which neither die nor sleep, but are immortal, return to God. The righteous are made perfect and enter heaven and the presence of God, awaiting the resurrection of the body, which is part of redemption. The souls of the wicked pass into a state of punishment for their sins. The existence of purgatory as an intermediate state is denied. There are only heaven and hell. Finally there will be a day of judgment, when the bodies of the dead will be raised to honor or dishonor. The resurrected bodies will be similar to the body of the risen Christ.

"Finally will come the 'Last Judgment,' with Christ as the judge. The whole world will be judged, included apostate angels, and they will be judged according to their thoughts, words, and deeds. The judgment will reveal God's mercy to those who are saved and his justice in punishing sin. The righteous will go into everlasting life, and the wicked who have refused to accept the salvation offering in the gospel will be punished for their sins. The warning of the day of judgment is to deter men from their sin and to comfort the godly in their adversity" (Miller, pp. 69-70).

E. Disciples of Christ

Generally, the Disciples of Christ hold to the immortality of the soul, coming judgment of the righteous and wicked, and eternal life for the righteous and eternal damnation for the wicked. The premillennial view would not be typical.

F. Latter Day Saints

Article 10 of the Articles of Faith states: "We believe in the literal gathering of Israel and in the restoration of the Ten Tribes; that Zion will be built upon this [the American] continent; that Christ will reign personally upon the earth; and, that the earth will be renewed and receive its paradisiacal glory."

This passage suggests and other "Mormon prophecies" confirm that the Latter Day Saints believe that both the Jews and the 10 Lost Tribes of Israel will be gathered to Palestine before the Lord returns. Moses is said to have appeared in person to Joseph Smith to give him and his followers "the keys of the gathering of Israel" (*Doctrine and Covenants*, 110:11).

Smith also prophesied that the Latter Day Saints will be gathered "to stand upon Mount Zion, which shall be the city of New Jerusalem. Which city shall be built, beginning at the temple lot, which is appointed by the finger of the

Lord, in the western boundaries of the State of Missouri, and dedicated by the hand of Joseph Smith, Jun., and others with whom the Lord was well pleased. Verily this is the word of the Lord, that the city of New Jerusalem shall be built by the gathering of the saints, beginning at this place, even the place of the temple, which temple shall be reared in this generation. For verily this generation shall not all pass away until an house shall be built unto the Lord, and a cloud shall rest upon it, which cloud shall be even the glory of the Lord, which shall fill the house" (*Doctrine and Covenants*, 84:2-5). Of course, no such building was built by Joseph Smith in Missouri in that generation, nor has it ever been built. Moreover, this teaching indicates that "after Christ has returned to earth, there will be two capitals over which He shall reign during the millennium: Zion (or Independence, Missouri) on the American Continent; and Jerusalem in Palestine" (Hoekema, p. 68).

The Mormons also teach that as Christ returns, the believing dead will be raised to meet Christ in the air and then will descend with Him. The believers who are alive, will, likewise, be caught up and then descend with Him. At the beginning of the thousand years, all the wicked shall be burned as stubble and their spirits will remain in the prison-house of the world where they can repent and cleanse themselves through suffering. Much time during the thousand years will be spent in baptizing for the dead. (See *Doctrine and Covenants* 29:9; 88:96-97; and Hoekema, pp. 69-70).

At the end of the thousand years, the wicked dead will be raised and there will be four different eternal abodes: (1) the *lake that burns with fire and brimstone* for "the sons of perdition" who were partakers of the Lord's power but who have denied the truth and defied His power; (2) the *telestial heaven* for those who were wicked and not raised for the millennium and for those who say they are "of Paul, and of Apollos, and of Cephas," who cannot marry or have children; (3) the *terrestial heaven* for those who died without law, those who did not receive Christ's testimony on earth but did accept it afterwards, honorable men who were blinded, and some others; (4) the *celestial heaven* (located on the renewed earth), the highest state, only for faithful Latter Day Saints who have made celestial marriages and who can, in this heaven, have mates and produce "spirit" children and advance into the state of gods themselves. These heavens are explained in *Doctrine and Covenants*, Section 76, and are further explained in Hoekema, pp. 71-74).

G. Jehovah's Witnesses

As studied earlier, the Jehovah's Witnesses believe that when a person dies, he has *no soul that continues to live.* He is completely dead until such time as he may be resurrected. In their view, *Hades* refers only to the grave and when men die they simply enter the grave, not a place of departed spirits (*Let God Be True,* pp. 89-90). Members of the "anointed class" have been or will be resurrected with *spiritual bodies* and will become a part of the 144,000 who will actually go to heaven. Members of the "other sheep," however, as well as the great majority of mankind, will be raised with *physical bodies* during the millennium (See Hoekema, p. 294).

In 1914, according to the Jehovah's Witnesses, *Jesus "returned."* By this, however, they do not mean what is usually understood by His return. They believe that World War I was the fulfillment of a sign Christ gave in Matthew 24 and was the time when he "returned" in the sense that he *began to reign in heaven.* Prior to that time he had been in heaven but not sitting on a throne. In 1914 he ascended to His throne in heaven and thus began His second coming or "second presence." In 1918, Christ *cleansed his temple* which is described in *From Paradise Lost* as ridding the Jehovah's Witnesses of those with "selfish hearts and wrong ideas" (p. 213). According to *The Truth Shall Make You Free,* however, the temple cleansed was in heaven (pp. 303-304). After this cleansing of His temple, Christ then raised *some* of those from the anointed class who had died and took them to *heaven* to reign with Him (*From Paradise Lost,* p. 213). This is further explained as follows in *Let God Be True.* In 1918, when Christ came to *cleanse His temple,* the "living anointed Christians on earth could not precede those who had fallen asleep in death, but they have to keep on maintaining their integrity until their own death. When this remnant on earth die, they do not have to sleep awaiting their Master's return, but receive an immediate change to spirit life. They cease their earthly labors, but their service from then on continues without weariness—1 Thessalonians 4:15, NW, I Corinthians 15:51, 52; Revelation 14:13" (p. 203). This *transformation of these "anointed class" Christians* who have died into spirit beings is called "the first resurrection" and is only for those who will become part of the 144,000 in heaven. This teaching is not that their physical bodies will be raised, but that they are "re-created" or restored to life in a different form (*Make Sure of All Things,* p. 311; *Let God Be True,* pp. 275-282).

Summarizing the view of the Jehovah's Witnesses, thus far, we have the following time-table:

1914—Christ returned (began to reign in heaven)
1918—Christ cleansed His temple (removed from the Jehovah's Witnesses those who were in error)
—dead anointed (of the 144,000) given life again and taken to heaven

The next element in the doctrine of last things suggested by the Jehovah's Witnesses is *a twofold judgment* to begin in 1918. The *first element* of this judgment is within the "house of God" as God distinguishes between His true and His false followers. The *second element* of judgment to begin in 1918 is the "judgment of the nation" which consists of the separation mentioned in Matthew 25 of dividing the *sheep* and the *goats*. This judgment lasts from the spring of 1918 until the Battle of Armageddon and during this judgment those who have "no appreciation for God's kingdom but reject the Kingdom message and its bearers and show them no help or kindness" will be *goats* and will be destroyed in the Battle of Armageddon. Those to be considered *sheep*, on the other hand, are those who "rejoice at the Kingdom's coming and do good to the remnant or last members of 'Christ's body' on earth." These will be spared in the Battle of Armageddon (*Let God Be True*, p. 290).

During the lifetime of the generation on earth in 1952, the Battle of Armageddon will come (*Let God Be True*, p. 179). This battle will be fought between the forces of evil, including Satan and his angels, the national governments of the world, religious heads of heathen religions and false Christian religions, and all the goats who have been separated by the judgment, on one side, while on the other are the forces of righteousness led by Christ and including those in the 144,000 left on earth, the other sheep, and the angels of heaven (*You May Survive Armageddon*, pp. 338-339). This will be the most terrible battle in history with *Satan's forces* using all their military, naval, and air equipment, including atomic power while *Christ* will use natural forces such as floods, earthquakes, hailstones, fires, flesh-eating plagues. Christ, of course, will win with over two billion people being killed (*You May Survive Armageddon*, pp. 337-343).

Only faithful Jehovah's Witnesses will survive and those will start to reign with Christ for a thousand years. The 144,000 will remain *in heaven* to reign there even while

Christ is on earth. On *earth* reigning with Christ will be *those who have survived* in the Battle of Armageddon and *those who will be raised or re-created* to have a part in the thousand-year period. First there will be the "resurrection of life" which includes those faithful during Old Testament times and "other sheep" who died before Armageddon. This resurrection of life is then followed by the "resurrection of judgment," spread out in time, when those who wanted to do right but did not have enough knowledge will be given *another opportunity*. Children will be born during this period to the "other sheep." All those alive for part or all of the millennium will under go judgment on the basis of their lives *during the millennium only*. If they are approved, they will receive the right to eternal life but if they are not approved, then they will be finally annihilated (*From Paradise Lost*, pp. 228-232 and Hoekema, pp. 314-321).

At the end of the thousand years, during which Satan has been bound, he will be loosed to make a final attempt to overcome the forces of good, and some will be led astray (*Let God Be True*, p. 270). Satan and all of his forces will then be cast into the lake of fire which means their complete annihilation (*Let God Be True*, pp. 270, 293).

Now, since all the wicked are now non-existent, the final state of the righteous begins. The "other sheep," who pass the judgment during the millennium, will remain forever on the renewed *earth*, while the 144,000 will live forever with Christ in *heaven* (*Let God Be True*, p. 132 and Hoekema, pp. 324-325).

H. Seventh-day Adventists

Like the Jehovah's Witnesses, Seventh-day Adventists also believe that at death a person passes entirely out of existence. There is not a "soul" that continues to live. From the time of one's death until his resurrection, then, he is in an "intermediate state" of non-existence. All human beings will, however, be raised at their appointed time to enter their final state. This belief is stated in Articles 9 and 10 of their Fundamental Beliefs.

Adventists believe in *three different resurrections*. The first one comes *prior* to the second coming of Christ and involves some who have been evil and some who have been good. The *evil ones* involved in this special resurrection are said to be those who pierced Christ (Revelation 1:7). The *good* said to be raised *prior* to the second coming are those who have died in the faith of the third angel's message (Revelation 14:9-13). He is said to have announced the requirement to observe the seventh day. Thus, all those faithful to the cause of the Seventh-day Adventists since 1846 will be raised to witness the second coming of Christ (See Hoekema, p. 139-140).

The Battle of Armageddon, in the view of the Adventists, will be the final conflict among nations and this will bring an end to world history. Fought in the plain of Megiddo in Palestine, this battle will be a "holy war" between God and His followers and Satan with his followers. The war will be climaxed by the second coming of Christ who will personally and visibly come to break the nations to pieces with a rod of iron. All the unrighteous who have not been killed in the Battle will be put to death and Satan will be "bound" in the sense that he will be confined to the earth. All the wicked are now dead.

Now comes the second resurrection. All the righteous who died prior to 1846 and those in the Lord since 1846 who had not known of the truth of the third angel, will now be brought back to life and will go to heaven to reign with Christ for a thousand years. This leaves the earth desolate except for Satan who will be alone there serving as a "scapegoat" in the wilderness. All believers who are still alive when Christ returns will be transformed and go with these resurrected to heaven.

During the thousand years, the righteous in heaven will be assisting Christ in judging the unrighteous to determine "the amount of punishment due each sinner for his part in the rebellion against God" (*Questions on Doctrine*, pp. 496-498).

Now comes the third and final resurrection of dead ones. *At the end of the thousand years*, the wicked dead, who have been in a state of non-existence, will now be given life again and begin to spread over the earth, having the same rebellious spirit as before. Satan is loosed now for the "little season" and takes over the host of resurrected wicked. These now attack "the new Jerusalem" which has come down out of heaven which means that *all the human race* now meets in one final confrontation—the wicked against the righteous. This battle, to be distinguished from Armageddon at the beginning of the millennium, results in the final defeat of Satan. All the wicked will now be annihilated but each will first have a period of suffering the length of which is equated to his guilt. Satan is the last to perish. In the final conflagration which destroys Satan and his hosts, the *earth* is cleansed and will become the eternal home of the righteous (See Hoekema, pp. 140-143).

I. Assemblies of God

According to Riggs, pages 122 to 131, the following events are *soon* to unfold. Since some have departed from the faith, and since there has been a great falling away and denial of cardinal doctrines of the church, and since the Jews have returned to Palestine, and since there is a United Nations which can become the Federation of the Nations over which the Anti-christ will rule, and since the world now has the power to destroy half of mankind, we know that we are in the *last days*. Just ahead, therefore, is the *Great Tribulation* which shall be a terrible ordeal for all who are living on the earth then. Fortunately, the Lord will descend from heaven in the clouds and *catch away* both the living and dead who are "in Christ" for the *Rapture of the Saints*. Thus, during the *Great Tribulation*, all of Christ's followers will be in heaven with Jesus. At this time is the "bema judgment" of Romans 14:10 when those taken into heaven in the rapture will be *judged* according to the deeds done in the flesh (II Corinthians 5:10). Toward the end of the tribulation, Christ and all His redeemed in heaven will celebrate the Marriage Supper of the Lamb.

As the tribulation nears its end, *The Battle of Armageddon* will occur as the last great battle of this dispensation when the Anti-christ and all the armies of the world are gathered to fight against Christ. The Anti-christ and the false prophet will be taken alive and be cast into the lake of fire and all his soldiers will be slain.

Jesus and His army will take over the government of the world as the *thousand-year reign* begins. At this time, representatives of all nations will be gathered before Christ in Jerusalem and He will *judge* them according to their treatment of His people, the Jews, who by this time have accepted Christ. The *nations* who have been kind to Jews will be allowed to go into His kingdom intact but those who have been unkind will be dissolved as nations and their leaders sent to hell (Matthew 25:31-46). At this point, Jesus will now establish a righteous government on earth and there shall be peace for a thousand years. A *temple* will be built in Palestine which will be the religious center of the world and the Jews will be the leading nation of the earth. "The curse will be lifted from nature and wild animals will be tame."

At the end of the thousand years, the *devil will be released* from the bottomless pit, where he was placed after Armageddon, and God will gather out of His Kingdom everything that offends and will burn it up with fire. The devil will, at this time, be cast into the Lake of Fire. The wicked will then be *judged* before the *Great White Throne* and the world shall be purified by fire to prepare it for eternity. The *New Jerusalem* shall then come down out of heaven and God will live and reign with and over his people for ever.

J. Church of the Nazarene

"We believe that the Lord Jesus Christ will come again; that we who are alive at His coming shall not precede them that are asleep in Christ Jesus; but that, if we are abiding in Him, we shall be caught up with the risen saints to meet the Lord in the air, so that we shall ever be with the Lord.

"We believe in the resurrection of the dead, that the bodies of both the just and of the unjust shall be raised to life and united with their spirits—'they that have done good, unto the resurrection of life; and they that have done evil, unto the resurrection of damnation.'

"We believe in future judgment in which every man shall appear before God to be judged according to his deeds in this life.

"We believe that glorious and everlasting life is assured to all who savingly believe in, and obediently follow Jesus Christ our Lord; and that the finally impenitent shall suffer eternally in hell" (*Manual*, pp. 32-33).

The *Manual* makes no statement about the 1000-year reign.

Teaching of the Scripture on the Last Things

It is beyond the scope of this work to provide a complete statement of the teaching of the Scriptures on "last things" and a full refutation of the many errors included in the wide variety of doctrines contained in the beliefs just described. It will be helpful here, however, to provide a brief outline of the premillenial view often taken, a brief refutation of it, and then an explanation of some of the basic passages those wishing to discuss these matters with others should study and understand.

A view mentioned above in describing the position of some of the denominations is often referred to as "dispensational premillennialism." The outline following describes this view in brief. The statements in brackets present what the author believes to be the biblical view on each of these points.

The explanations of the passages that follow this outline will demonstrate how the author's view is supported by the correct interpretation of these passages.

1. Signs of the end—Matthew 24:4-24 gives a list of signs such as earthquakes, famines, wars, rumors of wars, persecution of Christians, the spread of Christianity, and others by which one can forecast when the end of the world is coming.

    [It is interesting that for hundreds of years, particularly since the mid-1800's, this passage has been used by some to predict that the "end of the world" was to come within a short time. Each round of war or earthquakes or persecution of Christians has been thought to be the fulfillment of this passage and, thus, a sign that the end was imminent. As each of these prophets, however, has been shown to be false, he or another just moves the date later. The truth of the matter is that this section of Matthew 24 is not speaking of the end of the world at all. As Jesus begins His discourse on the fall of Jerusalem, an event which would happen during the lifetimes of the generation to whom He was speaking (Matthew 24:34), He is warning those in Jerusalem not to be fooled into thinking that each time they hear of a war or an earthquake or persecution that His prediction about the fall of Jerusalem is immediately upon them. Rather, the real sign by which they will know it is time to leave the city is "when ye see Jerusalem surrounded by armies," a fulfillment of Daniel's "abomination of desolation" (Matthew 24:15; Luke 21:20). So not only is this passage *not* about the end of the world, it is a list of events which Jesus says are *not even to be taken as signs* of the event of which He speaks—the fall of Jerusalem.]

2. The rapture—a moment in time when all living Christians will be transformed and all dead Christians will be raised and these, together, will be taken up into the sky to be with Jesus for a period of seven years. During this seven years, they will be safe in heaven while terrible events are taking place on earth. At the end of the seven years, Jesus will return to earth with those "raptured,"

quash the Battle of Armageddon, and establish His earthly kingdom headquartered in Jerusalem.

[The Bible never uses the word rapture and, in fact, never says Christians will go to heaven for seven years only to return to earth for a thousand years. Such a view is drawn from a misunderstanding of several passages explained below, particularly from I Thessalonians 4:13-17 and I Corinthians 15:50-53. Such a view contradicts several clear statements in the Scriptures. (1) I Corinthians 15:22-26 says that when Jesus returns He will raise those who are Christ's, yet this view has Christ raising those who are His seven years before His return. (2) John 6:40, 44, and 54 state that the righteous will be raised on the "last day," not seven years before Christ's return and a thousand and seven years before the end of time. (3) John 12:48 says that those who reject Jesus will be judged on the "last day," the same day John 6:40 says the righteous will be raised. Again this does not match the view of "the rapture" that Christians will be raised a thousand and seven years before the wicked will be judged. (4) John 5:28, 29, and other Scriptures, state that the righteous and the wicked will both be raised at the same time, not, as this premillennial view suggests, in a series of three resurrections spread over more than a thousand years.]

3. At the time of the rapture, according to a common premillennial view, two Anti-christs will sign a pact to rebuild the Jewish temple in Jerusalem and after it is rebuilt, there will begin to be terrible warfare in the land of Israel, involving three hundred million soldiers from Europe, Russia, China, and other parts of the world. This Battle of Armageddon will be centered in the valley near Megiddo and during it, Christ will return and establish His kingdom on earth.

    [(1) In only four passages in the Bible does the term "anti-Christ" appear: I John 2:18, 22; I John 4:3; and II John 7. In all of these John is discussing false spiritual teachers who deny that Jesus has come in the flesh. There were many such teachers and John says they already existed in his day. The Bible never speaks of an "anti-Christ" political leader who shall plunge the world into terrible war just before the second coming of Christ.

(2) Predictions based on Ezekiel and Zechariah that God will rebuild the Jewish temple and reinstitute the animal sacrifices of the Old Covenant misunderstand both the passages on which they are based and the strong language of the Books of Hebrews and Galatians. The predictions of the rebuilding of the temple were made while the Jews were in exile in Babylon and their temple in ruins. These prophets, often in figurative and poetic language, were encouraging these Jews by telling them that God would restore them to their land and allow them to rebuild their temple. These prophecies were all fulfilled in the period following the Babylonian captivity. The Book of Hebrews makes it clear that the priesthood of Aaron, under which the sacrifices of the Old Covenant had to be offered, has ended. Hebrews 4:11-25 states that Jesus could not have been an Aaronic priest because He was not of the tribe of Levi and so He was a priest of the order of Melchizedek. Both the Aaronic priesthood and the law of which it was a part have been done away so that something better, under Christ, might come. Saul, a king but not of the tribe of Levi, offered the sacrifices of the Old Covenant and was severely rebuked for it for he was not qualified. So, if the Aaronic priesthood has been done away, who could possibly offer the sacrifices of that covenant with God's approval? Christ could not and a king of Israel could not. Who could? That such Old Covenant sacrifices would begin to be offered again, even if for a different purpose, is entirely contrary to the teaching of Hebrews and to the message of Galatians where Paul fought so hard against those who sought to hold to Christ with one hand and the law of Moses with the other.

(3) The predictions about the terrible war just before the end of the world are, likewise, based on misunderstandings of Bible passages, particularly in Daniel and Revelation. While it is beyond the scope of this book to deal with these in detail, Daniel chapters 11 and 12 had primary reference to events which happened during

the four hundred years before Christ's coming, telling of wars between rulers of Egypt and Syria over the land of Palestine. These were fulfilled in amazing detail at that time and do not refer to wars just before the end of the world. The only reference in the Bible to "Armageddon" is in Revelation 16:16 where a dragon (Satan) and two beasts are said to send frogs out of their mouths to gather the kings of the world together to Armageddon. This highly symbolic account is in the midst of the story that God will destroy Satan's tool, the Roman Empire, which he has been using to try to persecute the church out of existence during its early years. Chapter 16 tells of the pouring out of the bowls of God's wrath on the beast (the Roman Empire) and its followers, particularly those involved in emperor worship (the second beast). As these see their plan for destroying the church by persecution about to fail and the Empire going down to defeat, they call on their vassal kings to make a final stand, symbolically represented by calling them to the place where many strategic battles in the Bible took place, the valley near Megiddo. This passage has no reference to the end of the world, much less to a great battle involving three hundred million soldiers in and near the small valley of Megiddo.

(4) The most basic mistake of premillennialism is its incorrect understanding about the nature of Christ's kingdom. It teaches that at Christ's first coming, He intended to set up an earthly kingdom but failed to do so when the Jews rejected Him. This teaching is false from three standpoints. First, Jesus did not fail to do what He came to do. His cry on the cross, "It is finished," was His testimony that He did what He came to do. He made a fuller statement of this point in Luke 24:44-46: "All things must needs be fulfilled, which are written in the law of Moses, and the prophets, and the psalms, concerning me. Then opened he their mind, that they might understand the scriptures; and he said unto them, Thus it is written, that the Christ should suffer, and rise again from the dead the third day; and that repentance and remission of sins should be preached in his name unto all the nations, beginning from Jerusalem." Second, the Old Testament prophecies did not foretell

a physical kingdom. While many of these use figurative language that might sound like a description of a physical kingdom, these must be understood in light of Christ's teachings about the nature of the kingdom that He was to establish—"My kingdom is not of this world"—John 18:36; "the kingdom of God is within you"—Luke 17:21; "There are some here of them that stand by, who shall in no wise taste of death, till they see the kingdom of God come with power"—Mark 9:1. Third, had Jesus come to be an earthly king, the Jews would not have rejected Him. In fact, John 6:15 records that when Jesus had fed the five thousand, He perceived that the people were going to take him by force "to make him a king," and He withdrew. Being such a king was never His intent. His work was to reconcile sinners to God so they could live eternally with Him; to be a king on earth and reign over the physical affairs of men has no place in this far more important work.

Now for an explanation of some of the passages that are most vital in discussing the premillennial view.

1. *Matthew 24*. One of the most frequently quoted chapters in regard to the end of the world is the 24th chapter of Matthew where such familiar phrases as "wars and rumors of wars," "earthquakes," "famines" are found. These are often used as *signs* by which one can tell when the end of the world is approaching and those denominations which make these predictions, either specifically or generally, usually include Matthew 24 among the passages on which such statements are based. An analysis of this chapter will show that it may be divided into ten sections as follows:

   a. *The occasion* (23:9—24:2) which includes, from chapter 23, Jesus' condemnation of the hypocrisy of the scribes and Pharisees states that the retribution for the blood of all the slain prophets will be heaped upon the generation which slays the Son of God. Also a part of the occasion comes from the disciples' desire to show Jesus the temple to which Jesus replied, "There shall not be left here one stone upon another, that shall not be thrown down."

b.   *The question* (24:3) which in Matthew has three parts but in the accounts in Mark 13 and Luke 21 the question has only two parts. If we let the parallel accounts interpret the question for us, then the disciples asked, "Tell us, when shall these things be? and what shall be the sign of thy coming, and of the end of the world?" Even though the question as stated in Matthew mentions "the end of the age," it is likely that the apostles used such phraseology in the context of the question as stated in Mark and Luke since they could well have thought of the destruction of the temple in such terms. Jesus does go on later in the chapter to discuss the end of the world, but *verse* 34 clearly states that everything mentioned prior to this verse must happen *before that generation would pass.* Thus, everything prior to verse 34 describes the *destruction of Jerusalem*, a direct answer to the question the apostles had posed.

c.   *The misleading and preliminary signs* (24:4-14) are listed as Jesus seeks to answer the question of *when* the temple will be destroyed. The list given here is *not* a list of signs when the end of the world will come; it is *not* even a list of signs for the destruction of the temple or of Jerusalem. It is, rather, a list of things which the followers of Christ are to let pass as *not* being immediate signs of the coming destruction. Christ says of these that the disciples are *not to be led astray by these* and it will not be until after such things as these happen that the end (destruction of Jerusalem) shall come.

d.   *The real sign* (24:15) which will be a warning that the destruction of Jerusalem is at hand will be the coming of *the abomination of desolation* which in Luke's account is said to be the surrounding of Jerusalem with armies (Luke 21:20).

e.   *What to do when the real sign comes* (24:16-20). Those who see the armies coming should *make an immediate escape*, not delaying even long enough to go inside the house to pack. It is mentioned that a departure would be harder to make quickly for those with small children, or if it is in winter or on a Sabbath (when the gates of the city would be closed). Such circumstances, of course, have no application to the end of the world for there is no fleeing from that.

f. *The nature of the coming event* (24:21-28) is described as one of great suffering and when deceivers would try to give a false hope to many. Again, such are a *perfect description of the tragic siege of Jerusalem* but *do not apply* to the end of the world for this event will be sudden and no one will be deceived about it when it happens.

g. *Striking events to follow immediately* (24:29-31) are suggested in figurative terms often applied to the fall of nations (Isaiah 13:10; 34:4, 5; Ezekiel 32:7, 8). Even the sentence about "the son of man coming on the clouds of heaven" can have the meaning that He was the agent bringing about this destruction and, in a non-personal way, was coming upon the clouds to carry out this prophecy. Matthew 16:28, Daniel 7:13, Matthew 26:64, and Revelation 1:7 all speak of such comings of Christ. It was also following the destruction of Jerusalem that Christ could more effectively send His messengers (angels) to all parts of the world to preach to all nations since the destruction of Jerusalem ended once and for all any special relationship between God and the Jews.

h. *"In this generation"* (24:32-35) *suggests that everything prior to this verse applies to the destruction of Jerusalem and its consequences.* The "generation of which Jesus speaks here is the generation then alive. Jesus' other uses of this word in Matthew will confirm this. So all spoken to this point in the chapter applies to the fall of Jerusalem.

i. *"But of that day and hour"* (24:36-40) is a clear change in thought. Now he is turning *from the destruction of Jerusalem to a discussion of the end of the world.* Notice the complete *contrast.* He has told them *when* the destruction of Jerusalem will be but "of that day and hour" *no one knows except God.* He has given them the *sign* of the destruction of Jerusalem, but "of that day and hour" there will be *no sign* to warn even as there was no sign to warn of the coming flood in Noah's day. He has urged them to *flee* from the destruction of Jerusalem, but "of that day and hour" there will be *no flight* for of two who are side by side in the field or at a mill, one will be taken and the other left. In Luke's account (21:35), the event described as "that day" is said to come, not on one city, but "upon all them that dwell on the face of the earth."

j.   *"Watch therefore"* (24:41-51) suggests that for the second coming, which no one can anticipate as to time, it is important to *be prepared* at all times. The 25th chapter continues this thought with the parables of the ten virgins, and the talents, and then the judgment account. Note how everything prior to verse 34 is well applied to the destruction of Jerusalem and everything starting with verse 36 clearly fits the second coming. These two events are put into *contrast* and the net result is not a list of signs by which we can predict when the second coming will be but rather a clear statement that since we cannot predict it, we should be ready at all times. For a fuller statement of this approach to Matthew 24 read the work of J. Marcellus Kik on this passage. Among other places it is in a collection of his works called *An Eschatology of Victory*, Presbyterian and Reformed Publishing Co., 1974. Also see the author's book called *Like a Thief in the Night* available at 21st Century Christian.

2.   *I Corinthians 15:34.* This passage places in order the events which will occur at the return of Christ: (1) prior to that time, *Christ himself will have been raised* from the grave; (2) then when Christ returns, *those that are His will be raised* from the dead; (3) then comes *the end* when Christ shall *give His kingdom back* to God for all authority will be abolished and all enemies destroyed including death. From this order, several things are apparent: (1) *the dead will be raised* when Christ returns and this will give Him the victory over death (if not all dead were raised then, He would not have a complete victory over death); (2) *He has been reigning* prior to His coming and at that time *He will end*, not begin, His reign; (3) when He returns, an *end*

will come, not the beginning of a thousand-year reign; (4) when He returns, He will *give the kingdom to God*, not start a new one.

3. *I Corinthians 15:50-54.* This passage states that some will be alive when Christ returns and these shall be *changed without death* into their new body while those who have been buried will come forth with their new bodies. Notice in verse 42 that the body which "is raised" is the same body that was "sown." Verse 52 says that this *change* for those who have died will be at "the last trump," thus indicating that the resurrection is not preceding a thousand-year reign but at the end of time, at the sounding of the last trumpet.

4. *I Thessalonians 4:13-18.* Those who believe in the "rapture" or snatching away of the righteous into heaven for a seven-year period prior to the second coming, base such an idea primarily on this passage. They say that the words "the dead in Christ shall rise first" mean that the righteous dead shall be raised before the *wicked dead* and will join Christ in the air. Seven years later, these who have been taken to heaven will return to earth to reign with Christ for a thousand years and, after that, the wicked dead will be raised.

If we ask what question Paul is answering, we will recognize that such is not intended in this passage. He is answering the question of *whether those Christians who are alive when Christ returns will be in a better state than those who have died before that time.* The answer is that "the dead in Christ shall rise first" and then those who are alive will be caught up with them into the air, and so shall they ever be with the Lord. This passage does not describe what will happen to the *wicked dead.* It neither states that they will or will not be raised when the *righteous dead* will be. Rather, the comparison here is between the *good dead* and the *good living.* We have to learn from *other passages* about when the wicked dead will be raised. The passage, however, leaves no room for a seven-year period and a thousand-year reign for it says that after the righteous (living and dead) are caught up into the air to meet the Lord, so shall they be with Him forever. Certainly nothing is said of their coming back to earth with Him for a thousand years.

5. *John 5:28, 29.* These verses do speak to the question of whether there will be *more than one resurrection,* one or more for the righteous and one or more for the wicked. "The *hour* cometh when all that are in the tombs shall hear his voice, and shall come forth; they that have done good, unto the resurrection of life; and they that have done evil, unto the resurrection of judgment." Since both the righteous and the wicked are said to come forth from the tombs when *"the hour cometh,"* this is a clear indication that they will come out of the tombs *at the same time.* Further, those who are wicked and those who are righteous will be divided at that time with each sent to his eternal abode.

6. *John 6:40, 44, 54.* These verses all mention that the resurrection of the righteous will be on *"the last day."* Now if the righteous are raised on *the last day,* then there is no place for a thousand years of days after the righteous are raised before the wicked are raised and the final judgment comes.

7. *II Thessalonians 1:7, 8.* Some teach that when Christ returns, He will set up a kingdom and then, after a thousand years, will punish the wicked. This passage, however, says that when Christ returns, He will come in flaming fire to render "vengeance to them that know not God, and to them that obey not the gospel of our Lord God, and to them that obey not the gospel of our Lord Jesus: who shall suffer punishment, even eternal destruction from the face of the Lord." Again, no room for a thousand-year reign when He returns and a clear statement that the wicked will have an eternal destruction.

8. *Matthew 25:46.* Following the passage about the judgment in which the sheep and goats will be separated, the Lord says the wicked "shall go away into eternal punishment: but the righteous into eternal life." From this verse we learn that the *punishment of the wicked* and the *life* of the righteous will both last the *same length of time.* There will not be the extinction of the wicked.

9. *Revelation 20.* This passage is the only one in the Scriptures to mention a "thousand year reign." But to what reign does it refer? One studying this passage must remember that he/she is coming to the

end of a book filled with figures and symbols—seven-headed dragons, ferocious beasts, lambs with seven eyes and seven horns, locusts with faces like men and hair like women, horses with heads like lions and tails like scorpions. The story of the Book of Revelation is real but the pictures used to tell the story are symbolic. We must understand that the book has two levels—the symbolic upper level and the real message which lies beneath. With this in mind, we look at the symbolic picture in Revelation 20 and then at the real message which it is intended to convey.

Revelation 20:4-6 does speak of a thousand-year reign. Answering four questions about this reign, however, will help us to know what the underlying message of the writer is. (1) *Who will reign?* Those pictured on thrones reigning with Jesus are said to be those beheaded for their testimony of Jesus and who did not have the mark of the beast. The beast in Revelation represents the Roman Empire, a world-wide empire which existed in the time when this book was written, situated on seven hills, and persecuting the church (Revelation 13:5-7; 17:9, 10). So those who are here pictured as reigning with Christ are the souls of those who were killed for testifying of Jesus and who refused to worship the emperors of the Roman Empire. These martyrs are part of the story throughout the book of Revelation—6:9-11; 7:9-17; 14:1-5; 15:2-4; 19:1, 2, 14. So, who reigns with Christ for a thousand years? The passage says that it is the souls of those who died for the testimony of Jesus during the terrible Roman persecution of the church. (2) *Why are they said to reign?* The Book of Revelation was delivered to churches soon to be plunged into terrible persecution by Rome. To encourage them to "be faithful unto death," Christ assured them that if they would be faithful to Him by giving their lives for His cause, they would be with Him to celebrate their great victory after their cause survives and Rome goes to defeat. The picture of "reigning with Christ for a thousand years" is a symbolic way of suggesting their great reward which will follow their suffering. (3) *Where will this reign be?* There is no suggestion in the passage that it is to be on earth. The picture is a heavenly one—of Christ and the souls of Christian martyrs in a heavenly reign with Christ. After all, those reigning are pictured as souls—after death and not yet in a resurrected body. Throughout the book, the martyrs have been in heaven and so has Christ. (4) *When will the reign be?* The reign starts in chapter 20, just following the defeat of the two beasts at the end of chapter 19. Thus, when the two beasts (the Roman Empire and the Cult of Emperor Worship) go down to defeat, the reign begins. After Satan's tool for seeking to persecute the early church out of existence is gone, the reign begins. The celebration signified by the "thousand year reign" lasts until the end of time, except for the little time of Revelation 20:7-10. So the reign started about 475 A.D. with the fall of the Roman Empire and is pictured as lasting until the second coming, except for the brief time when Satan meets his final destruction.

Even if we do not agree entirely on the meaning of these symbols, it is clear that the reign is not on earth, is by souls not bodies, is a special reward for those early martyrs, other Christians not even being in the picture. Since I Corinthians 15:22-26 makes it clear that Christ reigns before His return and then gives the kingdom back to God, the reign of Revelation 20 could not be after Christ's return.

The thousand years is a symbolic period in the midst of a symbolic book. While there may never be agreement among all students of the Bible as to what the thousand years symbolizes, it is certainly not a description of a literal reign of Christ and resurrected saints on earth from Jerusalem. See commentaries on Revelation by J.W. Roberts, Homer Hailey, Rubel Shelly, and Ray Sommers for more on this passage. See also the author's book *Unlocking Revelation* available at 21st Ceutury Christian.

Section II
Islam

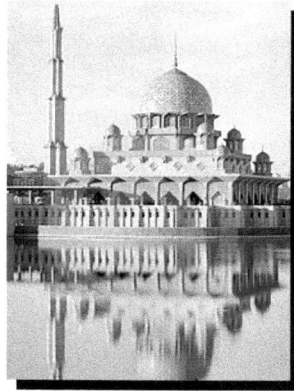

The Religion of Islam

The religion of Islam, started in 622 A.D. by Mohammad, now has more than a billion adherents throughout the world. Estimates of the number in the United States vary from 2 to 7 million, depending on who gives the numbers. This religion has come to particular prominence since September 11, 2001, when Muslim terrorists crashed airplanes into the World Trade Center and the Pentagon. Certainly everyone interested in knowing about religions of the 21st century must know something about this religion: where did they come from, what do they believe, what is their goal, and how can Christians best approach them?

This section is intended to give a brief response to these questions. The information here is taken primarily from Glover Shipp's book *Christianity and Islam*, published by Covenant Publishing in 2002. For more details, consult this book and other sources to which he refers.

A Brief History of Islam

In 622 B.C., Mohammad was living in Mecca, on the Arabian Peninsula. He was a trader and the husband of a rich widow. He claimed to have had a series of visions from Gabriel starting in 610. From these visions, which he said continued for more than twenty years, he proclaimed a new religion which included a belief in some of the stories of the Old Testament such as those of Abraham and Moses. He also said Jesus was a prophet, but was neither the Son of God nor the last of God's great prophets.

The people of Mecca did not receive Mohammad's claims well because he was teaching monotheism while they believed in a pantheon of gods. For safety, he had to flee to Medina. There he was more favorably received and began to promote his new religion called Islam, which means submission to Allah. Soon the city of Medina, following Mohammad's plan, became a theocracy. Using armed forces and persuasion, Mohammad began to spread his religion to other places and by 630, he was strong enough to attack the city of Mecca and force them to surrender. He threw out the idols from their temple but retained the temple and a large black stone they had used in their worship of idols and made this city the center of his religion. Many of the Arabian tribes submitted to his authority but in 632, Mohammad died. At this point, scribes had written down some of Mohammad's revelations and so his friend, Abu Bekr, ordered that these "revelations from Gabriel" should be collected into what is now called the Qur'an or Koran.

After Mohammad's death, even though there were disputes over who would be the new leaders, the religion continued to spread. By the 15th century the religion had conquered all the way to Spain and other parts of Europe, North Africa, central Russia, and in the other direction, to India, Malaysia, and Indonesia. Much of this expansion came by military force. Mohammad had taught that any of his followers who died in battle for the faith was assured of entrance into Paradise. In some places, however, the submission was peaceful since Christians and Jews were promised that they could continue to observe their own religion.

There are many divisions among the Muslims. Soon after the death of Mohammad, there began to be strife between those who sought to be his successor. Eventually those called Sunnis became the majority. These take the Qur'an a little less strictly than some others. The primary sect of Islam opposing them are the Shi'ites who comprise about 15 percent of the total today. These live primarily in Iran with some in Iraq. The Shi'ites are more militant and hold that all other branches of Islam are in error.

The Basic Beliefs of Islam

1. First and foremost, all Muslims believe in Allah as the one true God.
2. They also believe that Mohammad was the final, great prophet of God, surpassing all other prophets.

3. They believe the Qur'an is the revealed truth from God through Gabriel and, as such, it supersedes all other prophecies. It is a collection of visions to Mohammad which deal with personal, moral, religious, and civil matters. It is divided into 114 chapters or Suras, arranged according to their length. There is no particular sequence and it is highly poetic in its use of imagery. Muslims believe the Qur'an supersedes the Old Testament and the New Testament and where they are in disagreement, it is because they believe the Bible has been corrupted. So the word of the Qur'an prevails. This means that when one quotes the Bible to a Muslim, he may well say this passage is part of where the Bible has been changed.

4. Muslims summarize their duties in five pillars or foundational duties.

    a. Confession. At least five times a day the faithful Muslim will chant these words, "I testify that there is no God but Allah and Mohammad is His prophet." "Allah" is the Arabic word for "god."

    b. Prayer. Five times a day all Muslims are to pray: early morning, noon, mid-afternoon, sunset, and evening. Anyone who has visited a Muslim country can testify to hearing the call to prayer now done by loud-speakers from the towers of mosques. Each person stops what he/she is doing, falls prostrate toward Mecca and prays. At the Friday noon hour of prayer, they assemble at a mosque for prayer and a lesson from their "preacher."

    c. Almsgiving. All Muslims are to share some of their income and goods with those in need. This is a type of "religious tax" all are expected to pay.

    d. Fasting. Mohammad designated the month of Ramadan as a month of fasting. During this time, all are expected to refrain from eating food between sunrise and sunset. This fast, held as an honor to the Qur'an, is used as time to develop self-control.

    e. The Pilgrimage. Every Muslim who is physically able to do so is to visit Mecca at least once in a lifetime. Typically they save for years to have the funds to make this trip. Once in Mecca they fulfill certain rituals including touching the black stone and living in a tent for several days. Having made the trip, a Muslim is entitled to wear a special white cap.

f. Some Muslims add a sixth pillar: jihad or holy war. The word means struggle—first an inner struggle and then an outer struggle against "infidels." If Muslim leaders declare a "jihad," then it is right to wage "holy war" against infidels, even to the point of bloodshed. There are statements in the Qur'an about killing "infidels" although some Muslims say their religion is really a peaceful one. The history of Islam, however, shows that it was often spread by force and that many Muslims are incited to violence by their leaders. Some today say it is only the Muslim extremists who use violence and while they certainly do, other Muslim leaders have not been very forceful in condemning such violence. Certainly not all Muslims approve of the terrorist tactics that some are using.

Muslims are also expected to abstain from pork and alcoholic beverages. They may, however, use tobacco and stronger addictive drugs. Polygamy is permitted, allowing a man to have as many as four wives if he can support them and the children. Adultery, stealing, blaspheming the name of Allah, and failure to keep the five pillars are all considered violations of the Muslim law and make one the subject of punishment including severe physical punishment.

It is also against their law for a Muslim to convert to Christianity or Judaism and where they control the government, it is unlawful for Christians to seek to convert Muslims. Their governments will sometimes allow Christian families to practice their religion in private but forbid them to "proselytize" Muslims.

Muslims do not believe in separation of church and state. To them, a government based on Muslim principles and laws is the best way for people to keep the principles of the Qur'an. Their ultimate goal is to have all governments controlled by Muslims so their religion would be practiced by everyone in the world.

The Muslims believe in heaven and hell and think Allah will eventually judge everyone.

Observations

1. The God "Allah" of the Muslims is different from the God "Jehovah" of the Christians. Muslims deny the concept of the Trinitarian God saying that such is not true monotheism. In fact, they say that the Bible passages used to support the doctrine of the Trinity, such as Matthew 3:16 and John 14:25-16, are corruptions of the Scripture.

2. They also deny that Jesus is "God in the flesh." They regard Jesus as a prophet and even born of a virgin, but they deny His claim to be the Son of God. Christians, of course, see in this a contradiction because, they say, if Jesus is not part of the Godhead, then He lied about who He is and must be regarded as a false prophet. (See John 3:36; Matthew 16:18.) Muslims deny that Jesus was killed on a cross. They believe Jesus only "appeared" to die and that perhaps someone else died there and that Jesus was just taken up to heaven. They believe He will return later to die and to be raised from the dead along with everyone else.

3. Muslims have used violence as a way to spread their faith. Mohammad led an armed assault on Mecca and much of the spread of Islam in the early centuries involved armed conflict. This is in contrast to the teachings of Jesus who never permitted violence in His cause. While some Christians, as in the Crusades, have mistakenly taken up violence in the name of the religion, the founder certainly never taught or encouraged any such practice. One can only become a Christian by making a personal choice to believe and obey Jesus (Mark 16:16; Acts 2:38; Acts 8:12).

4. One becomes a Muslim in one of two ways. Most are just born into a family which follows Islam and, at the appropriate age, begins to observe the "pillars." Others decide to become followers of Mohammad and confess Allah as the one true God and Mohammad as His prophet, thus becoming participants in Islam. There is not an experience in Islam that parallels the Christian "conversion" with certain rites one must follow (Romans 6:4; Galatians 3:27).

5. Muslims believe that they will be saved by observing the "pillars." If one follows generally the teachings of the Muslim faith then they have

reason to expect that they will eventually go to the gardens of paradise. Muslims do not believe that any "sacrificial death," such as Jesus on the cross, is needed. Christians, on the other hand, believe in salvation by grace through an obedient faith (Ephesians 2:8-9; Romans 1:5).

6. Many Muslims are very dedicated to their religion and are willing even to die for it. Even those who disagree with them must admire such dedication. Many Christians, of course, have died for their faith as well, both in ancient and modern times, many of these submitting to horrible deaths rather than deny their faith in Jesus Christ.

Reaching Out to Muslims

Since the Muslims think about things quite differently than Christians do, it is not easy to find a point of engagement. The things suggested below can, however, help bridge the gap and provide a starting place. Of course, as in all personal discussions about religion with our friends, we do not want to be combative or unkind. We always want to speak with respect for the views of others, even when we disagree with them.

1. *Christian Living.* As with all people we seek to reach, our lives of kind service, good morals, and good families can be an excellent attraction to others. As we have opportunity, we should befriend Muslims living in our neighborhoods and provide care for them when they need it. Our children and their children can become friends. We can invite them into our homes and let them see our good family life. If there are Muslims in our workplace, we can show interest and concern for them there. Often others will be shunning them so that if we treat them with kindness, it will certainly be noticed. We will want to be careful of how we speak about the world situation in their presence and should avoid seeing all Muslims as terrorists. Letting our light shine is always an excellent way to engage those who are not Christians (Matthew 5:16).

2. *Honor God.* To the Muslim, honor is a very important virtue. They hold their God and the prophet Mohammad in high honor. They would never think of doing anything in disrespect. This is why even cartoons which, in their minds, show disrespect to Mohammad, are taken so seriously. We can appreciate their code of honoring what they hold to be important and show them that we also honor and respect our God (Hebrews 13:15; Revelation 4:8) and His prophet Jesus Christ (Revelation 5:11-12). We should never do anything by word or deed that would show disrespect.

3. *Help them understand Jesus.* Since the Qur'an teaches that Jesus is a prophet, we can, as we can find opportunity, use that as a starting point to help them know more about Him. Learn what the Qur'an says about Jesus and help the Muslim to know the Jesus of the New Testament, His life, His teachings, and His death. We can also teach them about the resurrection of Jesus and the promise that gives of eternal life (John 14:1-7). We can help them see the difference between what they have seen of Jesus through Muslim eyes and the Jesus we see in the Christian view.

4. *Show your Muslim friends the place of "love" in the Christian plan.* Explain to them about the greatest commandment (Matthew 22:34-40) and what this means in Christian living (John 15:9-17). Ask if this differs from the teachings of Islam.

5. *Tell the story of the Bible about sin and salvation in a simple, clear way.* Ask if you can present this story just to help your Muslim friends understand what the Bible teaches about the Christian plan of salvation (Romans 3:23; 6:23; John 3:16; Acts 22:16; Revelation 2:10). Even if they do not agree with it, you can seek to help them understand it. Tell your Muslim friends you would like to understand the way to heaven as the Muslims see it. Then you can compare the two.

6. *Share with your Muslim friend the story of Pentecost.* At an appropriate time in your conversations, share with your friends the story of Acts 2 where Peter gives the reasons to believe in Jesus as the Son of God and what our response to that should be. This will help them to see Christianity in its primitive form. Their view of it is conditioned by the Crusades and the many forms which it takes today. Helping them to

see that one can be a Christian as the early disciples did will make it easier for them to accept.

7. *Support mission efforts.* We can support efforts that churches and missionaries are making to reach out in the Muslim world. There is, for example, a Christian school operated by members of churches of Christ near Nazareth, Israel. Galilee Christian High School is a work of service and outreach in the midst of a Muslim community. Some believe the nation of Turkey is a good place to start reaching out since their government is less restrictive on religious activities and people may be a little less opposed to ideas from the West. As we become aware of efforts being put forth to reach out to Muslims, we should give them our support both financially and in prayer.

Conclusion

Since the Muslims constitute something like a fourth of the world population, their religion is certainly one to be acquainted with. Since all who come to the Christian faith must do it one-at-a-time, such is the way we must work with those who follow Islam. As we have opportunity to show them the good life to which Christ brings us and the hope He gives of eternity, we may be able to interest them in learning more about Christianity. While we should not paint all Muslims with the "terrorist" brush, the actions of some Muslims should cause some other Muslims at least to ask whether there is not a better way than the religion they have chosen.

Section III

Study Aids

This section of the book contains worksheets which can be used to summarize information contained in earlier chapters and to provide means to use the *Handbook* in a way to become more familiar with it. These materials can be used by an individual in his own study, by a class for homework to be discussed in class meetings, or as projects during a class meeting in small or large groups.

WORKSHEET 1—FOUNDING OF CHURCH

Fill in each blank, if possible. For some churches, of course, it will not be possible to complete each item. Do not force an answer if none fits.

Name of Church	Date Begun	Name of Founder or Early Leaders
Roman Catholic		
Baptist		
Methodist		
Presbyterian		
Disciples		
Mormons		
Jehovah's Witnesses		
Seventh-day Adventists		
Assemblies of God		
Nazarene		

Scriptures I wish to recall on this point:

WORKSHEET 2—GODHEAD

Mark with "Yes" if it is an accepted belief among all or the great majority of members; "Some" if it is allowed but not typical; "No" if it is generally opposed.

Name of Church	Believe in a godhead of three personalities— each equally divine.	Believe in the gifts of the Holy Spirit *today* in such actions as tongue-speaking or healing.
Roman Catholic		
Baptist		
Methodist		
Presbyterian		
Disciples		
Mormons		
Jehovah's Witnesses		
Seventh-day Adventists		
Assemblies of God		
Nazarene		
Bible teaching		
Scriptures I wish to recall on this point:		

WORKSHEET 3—NATURE OF MAN

Name of Church	Believe man has an immortal soul which lives forever.	Believe that the *guilt* of Adam's sin passes to all men as original sin.	Now believe in individual predestination to salvation.
Roman Catholic			
Baptist			
Methodist			
Presbyterian			
Disciples			
Mormons			
Jehovah's Witnesses			
Seventh-day Adventists			
Assemblies of God			
Nazarene			
Bible teaching			
Scriptures I wish to recall on this point:			

WORKSHEET 4—OLD COVENANT

Name of Church	Regard all of the Old Covenant as not binding on Christians.	Keep the Sabbath.
Roman Catholic		
Baptist		
Methodist		
Presbyterian		
Disciples		
Mormons		
Jehovah's Witnesses		
Seventh-day Adventists		
Assemblies of God		
Nazarene		
Bible teaching		
Scriptures I wish to recall on this point:		

WORKSHEET 5—SALVATION (1)

Name of Church	Teach salvation by faith only.	Baptize for remission of sins	Baptize infants	Baptize by Immersion only
Roman Catholic				
Baptist				
Methodist				
Presbyterian				
Disciples				
Mormons				
Jehovah's Witnesses				
Seventh-day Adventists				
Assemblies of God				
Nazarene				
Bible teaching				
Scriptures I wish to recall on this point:				

WORKSHEET 6—SALVATION (2)

Name of Church	Accept baptism from other churches regardless of manner or purpose	Believe in Holy Spirit baptism as necessary to salvation.	Believe in "sanctification" as a particular event separate from justification.	Believe in "once saved, always saved."
Roman Catholic				
Baptist				
Methodist				
Presbyterian				
Disciples				
Mormons				
Jehovah's Witnesses				
Seventh-day Adventists				
Assemblies of God				
Nazarene				
Bible teaching				
Scriptures I wish to recall on this point:				

WORKSHEET 7—ORGANIZATION

Name of Church	Consider themselves a denomination (part of the saved)	Organized at congregational level only	Highly-developed structure reaching to national or international level
Roman Catholic			
Baptist			
Methodist			
Presbyterian			
Disciples			
Mormons			
Jehovah's Witnesses			
Seventh-day Adventists			
Assemblies of God			
Nazarene			
Bible teaching			
Scriptures I wish to recall on this point:			

WORKSHEET 8—CHURCH

Name of Church	Requires baptism for church membership	Have a plurality of elders in each congregation	Employs a scriptural description as a designation
Roman Catholic			
Baptist			
Methodist			
Presbyterian			
Disciples			
Mormons			
Jehovah's Witnesses			
Seventh-day Adventists			
Assemblies of God			
Nazarene			
Bible teaching			
Scriptures I wish to recall on this point:			

WORKSHEET 9—WORSHIP

Name of Church	Any special doctrines on Lord's Supper	Women allowed to preach or lead in public worhip	Normally, how often take Lord's Supper
Roman Catholic			
Baptist			
Methodist			
Presbyterian			
Disciples			
Mormons			
Jehovah's Witnesses			
Seventh-day Adventists			
Assemblies of God			
Nazarene			
Bible teaching			
Scriptures I wish to recall on this point:			

WORKSHEET 10—LAST THINGS (1)

Yes=all or most members believe   Some=many members believe

No=none or few members believe

Name of Church	Believe in 1000-year reign on earth	Believe in more than one resurrection	Believe in more than one judgment	Believe in "the rapture"
Roman Catholic				
Baptist				
Methodist				
Presbyterian				
Disciples				
Mormons				
Jehovah's Witnesses				
Seventh-day Adventists				
Assemblies of God				
Nazarene				
Bible teaching				
Scriptures I wish to recall on this point:				

WORKSHEET 11—LAST THINGS (2)

Name of Church	Believe in punishment for wicked that never ends	Believe the eternal abode for righteous is on earth	Predict that end of the world is near
Roman Catholic			
Baptist			
Methodist			
Presbyterian			
Disciples			
Mormons			
Jehovah's Witnesses			
Seventh-day Adventists			
Assemblies of God			
Nazarene			
Bible teaching			
Scriptures I wish to recall on this point:			

WORKSHEET 12

Write your own definition of the following terms after you have studied them in the context of the various beliefs given in this study.

1. Original sin—

2. Premillennialism—

3. Rapture—

4. Denominationalism—

5. The Trinity—

6. Transubstantiation—

7. Justification—

8. "Born Again"—

9. Faith—

10. Repentance—

11. Water Baptism—

12. Baptism of the Holy Spirit—

13. Sanctification—

14. Perseverance of the Saints—

15. Miracle—

WORKSHEET 13

Points for Discussion

List under *each church* the two or three *points* you would like especially to discuss with a member of that group along with the *Scriptures* you would use and *principles* you would seek to establish.

Roman Catholic—

Baptist—

Methodist—

Presbyterian—

Disciples of Christ—

Latter Day Saints—

Jehovah's Witnesses—

Seventh-day Adventists—

Assemblies of God—

Nazarene—

Church of Christ—

WORKSHEET 14—ISLAM

Write a brief statement in response to the following questions about Islam.

1. When did Islam begin and who started it?

2. What book is the foundation of Islam and what is their understanding of how it was written?

3. What are the two main divisions among Muslims and how would you distinguish between them?

4. What are the five pillars of Islam and how would you describe each?

5. What is the relationship between the government and Islam in nations where Muslims are in control?

6. How does the Muslim concept of Allah differ from the Christian concept of the godhead?

7. What is the Muslim view of Jesus?

8. What is the Muslim view of how one can be approved to go to Paradise?

9. What are four ways you could actively reach out to share Christianity with a Muslim?

Suggestions for Teachers

In teaching this material, the teacher may wish to choose among or refine such objectives as these:

1. The student can explain briefly the history of the church from its beginning in New Testament times through the digression, the Reformation Movement, and the efforts to restore New Testament Christianity.
2. The student can explain the meaning of certain necessary terms in doctrinal study such as original sin, pre-millennialism, transubstantiation, the Trinity, baptism of the Holy Spirit, justification, perseverance of the saints, denominationalism, rapture, and miracle.
3. Using the *Handbook*, the student can state the belief of any church cited in this study on any major point of doctrine.
4. Using the *Handbook*, the student can state in his/her own words what the Bible teaches on various points of doctrine in this study.
5. Using the *Handbook*, the student can state whether he/she believes any particular statement of doctrine on the points covered is in harmony with Bible teaching on that subject.
6. The student will agree that what one believes religiously is important and will wish to continue to study carefully various points of doctrine.

The lesson plans are built around questions which the teacher can either use as points for lecture or which he/she may use as a springboard for class discussion. Sometimes the lesson plan calls for student reports drawn from their reading of the book or visits to local churches. The teacher may wish to include some role-playing experiences which allow students to "teach" each other on various points of doctrine. These are not included in the lesson plan but if time allows or if the teacher can make assignments for such activities between class meetings, they could be very profitable.

It is recommended that the teacher purchase the Teacher's Manual on *How to Explain* by the author of this book. It provides interesting and clear ways of explaining some points of doctrine which are covered in this *Handbook*. The teacher will wish to incorporate some of these methods of explanation in with the information available in this book. Some references are made to this Teacher's Manual in the lesson plans. This book is available through the 21st Century Christian Bookstore by calling 1-800-251-2477.

LESSON 1
HISTORY OF THE CHURCH—PART 1

Plan for the lesson:

1. Introduce the study by giving a brief overview of the book. Ask the students what values they see in such a study.

2. Introduce the topic of the first three lessons—some thoughts on church history. (The teacher will find the lesson on the Departure and Return in the Teacher's Manual of *How to Explain* to be a very helpful resource for these first three lessons. The use of the drawing presented there in more detail than in the *Handbook* will be of particular benefit.)

3. **Q:** Was the original plan for the teaching and practices of the church as revealed in the New Testament and in the approved practices of the early church intended to be the model for future generations? Or was each generation expected and allowed to make changes in these teachings and practices? (Refer to the following passages in this discussion: Acts 20:29-31; Galatians 1:6-9, 12; 1 Timothy 4:1-4; 2 Timothy 4:1-4; Jude 3.) We note from these passages two points: there was a body of truth called "the faith" or "the gospel" which all were to follow, and that there were predictions that people would stray from that body of teaching. We might represent this basic teaching which was set down for all to follow as a straight line running horizontally across the page.

4. **Q:** What are some changes that were made to the practices and doctrines of the church through the centuries and when were they made? Represent this with a line branching off of the original line.

5. **Q:** Who were some around the sixteenth century who pointed out that some of these changes were wrong and that the Catholic Church of that time should be reformed? What were some of the issues they raised and how were they treated? Represent this on the drawing by a branching off the "departure" line back toward the original line.

6. **Q:** What were the two main streams of the Reformation Movement? How are such churches as the Baptists, Presbyterians, and Lutherans related to these streams? When and how did the Methodists begin?

Assignment:

1. Read in the *Handbook* about the Disciples of Christ.
2. Complete what you can of the chart on the Founding of Churches

LESSON 2
HISTORY OF THE CHURCH—PART 2

Plan for the Lesson:

1. Consider together the chart on the founding of churches on what can be filled out to this point.

2. **Q:** What idea did people in different churches have in the late 1700's and early 1800's?

3. **Q:** When these learned of each other and began to work together, what movement did this create? **Q:** Who were some of the leaders? **Q:** What was their basic proposition?

4. **Q:** What happened in this movement following the Civil War? **Q:** On what issues were their differences? **Q:** What two approaches to Scripture do these reveal?

5. **Q:** What churches today are related to this movement? How do these differ?

6. **Q:** If one today follows the teaching of Peter on Pentecost, what church would he/she be a member of?

Assignment:

1. Read the information on the remaining churches covered in A Brief Sketch of Ten Churches.

2. Ask a different student to be prepared to give a six-minute report on the beginning and the teachings of the remaining churches to study.

LESSON 3
HISTORY OF THE CHURCH—PART 3

Plan for the Lesson:

(Call on the students to give their six minute reports and spend a couple of minutes highlighting the distinctive teachings.)

1. **Q:** How did the Seventh-day Adventist Church begin and what are some of their distinctive doctrines?

2. **Q:** How did the Church of Jesus Christ of Latter Day Saints (Mormons) begin and what are some of their distinctive doctrines?

3. **Q:** How did the Jehovah's Witnesses begin and what are some of their distinctive doctrines?

4. **Q:** How did the Assemblies of God begin and what are some of their distinctive doctrines?

5. **Q:** How did the Church of the Nazarene begin and what are some of their distinctive doctrines?

Assignment:

1. Complete the Worksheet on the Beginning of Churches.

2. Read the chapter on the Nature of God and be prepared to discuss what the Bible teaches on this topic.

3. Ask a different student to be prepared to present the doctrine of each of the ten churches on the nature of the Godhead. Some of these reports will be very brief if the church takes a biblical view on this point. If not, the report will be a little longer.

LESSON 4
THE NATURE OF GOD

Plan for the Lesson:
1. Review the Worksheet on the Beginning of Churches.
2. Ask each of the students assigned to present the view of each of the ten churches on the Nature of the Godhead.
3. Discuss what the Bible teaches on the following questions:
   a. **Q:** Does the Bible teach three separate but equal members of a Godhead?

   Use passages listed in the Handbook on this point.
   b. **Q:** What seems to be the distinctive role of each of the members of the Trinity? Look at John 5:30; Matthew 26:42; John 1:1-3; Colossians 1:15-17; John 16:13; 1 Corinthians 2:9; 2 Peter 1:21; Psalm 41:13.
4. Compare the teaching of Scripture with the following statements taken from the *Handbook.*
   a. "The Father has a body of flesh and bones as tangible as man's."
   b. "God was once a mortal man who passed through the school of earth-life similar to that through which we are now passing."
   c. "There was a time, wherefore, when Jehovah was all alone in universal space. All life and energy and thought were contained in him alone."
   d. "Christ is the highest of Jehovah's creation so also he was the first, direct creation of God."

Assignment:
1. Complete the worksheet on the Nature of God.
2. Read the following passages in preparation for the next lesson: Ezekiel 18:20; 1 Corinthians 15:20-28; Romans 3:23; 5:12; Psalm 58:7; Ephesians 2:3.

LESSON 5
THE FALL, ORIGINAL SIN, AND PREDESTINATION

Plan for the Lesson:

1. Discuss the teaching of Scripture on the following points. Be sure to use the Scriptures shown.

    a. Humans today are subject to death because of the sin of Adam but are not born guilty from the sin of Adam. Include a study of the following passages: Ezekiel 18:20; 1 Corinthians 15:20-28; Romans 3:23; 5:12; Psalm 58:7; and Ephesians 2:3.

    b. With the sin of Adam, human nature became corrupted and with a "positive inclination to sin." On their own, therefore, humans are unable to do the right thing. But, on the other hand, if we have a corrupted nature, are we responsible for being sinners? So, do we sin because we are corrupted or because we choose to sin? Am I a sinner because I choose to sin or because I can't help it?

    c. "We have all inherited the transgression of our first parents and that we are born enemies of God. And it is equally plain that these texts apply to every member of the human family—to the infant of a day old as well as to the adult." The passages given to support this view are Romans 5:12; Ephesians 2:3; Job 14:4 and Psalm 51:5. Do these passages support this view? Also consider passages under point "a" above.

2. The view of predestination is no longer held by many of the churches that once believed it. This view, for example, took Ephesians 1:4 to say that before the creation, God chose some individuals to be saved, leaving the others to be lost. This view held that those chosen by God to be saved could not be lost and those not chosen by God could not be saved. Most in the churches which once held this view hold it no longer. Discuss Ephesians 1:4 in the light of Ephesians 1:13, 2 Peter 3:9, Acts 10:34-35, and Revelation 22:17.

Assignment:

1. Using our study and other materials in the chapter, complete the worksheet on the Nature of Man.

2. Review the material in the *Handbook* on the inspiration and authority of Scripture. Be ready to discuss the various views.

LESSON 6
INSPIRATION AND AUTHORITY OF SCRIPTURE

Plan for the Lesson.

1. Review the worksheet on the Nature of Man.

2. From quotations in the *Handbook*, explain what is the view of Scripture in the following churches: Roman Catholic, Latter Day Saints, and the Jehovah's Witnesses.

3. **Q:** Is the Bible true because it has the marks of being more than a human work or because the Catholic Church has certified it as true?

4. A Catholic advertisement said, "The early church never saw the Bible." The statement suggests that since the New Testament books were not all collected until the fourth century, that the church existed before Scripture and so is more authoritative than Scripture. **Q:** So, which came first: the message of Scripture or the church?

5. **Q:** Which of the statements below is the best description of the "inspiration" of Scripture? Use the following passages in your discussion: John 16:13; 1 Corinthians 2:13; 2 Peter 1:20, 21; 2 Timothy 3:16, 17.

   a. God dictated every word to each writer of the Bible.

   b. The Holy Spirit gave writers the ideas and allowed them to put the message in their own words.

   c. The Holy Spirit sometimes revealed the exact wording and sometimes allowed the writers to use what they had seen and knew about, but oversaw the process so that all the words are "inspired" by the Holy Spirit.

6. Does God hold each person responsible for his/her understanding of and obedience to Scripture or does He expect us to accept without question the views of our church? Acts 17:11; Ephesians 1:13; Romans 10:13-15.

Assignment:

1. Read in the *Handbook* about the relationship of the two covenants.

LESSON 7
OLD AND NEW TESTAMENTS

Plan for the Lesson:

1. Study points 1 through 4 under what the Bible teaches on this point.

2. Some say that people living in the Christian age are no longer under the ceremonial or civil practices of the Old Testament but are still bound by the moral law including the ten commandments. **Q:** Is this the teaching of the New Testament? **Q:** How did Jesus treat the commandments of the Old Testament in the Sermon on the Mount? **Q:** Did He include any of them in His new law? **Q:** Did he change any of them? **Q:** Did he take any of them away?

3. Some say today we should look to the case of the thief on the cross as an example of how we can be saved today. They observe that the thief was not baptized and, therefore, baptism is not required for salvation. **Q:** Is this observation in harmony with what the New Testament teaches about the covenants?

4. **Q:** Are Matthew, Mark, Luke, and John part of the Old Covenant or the New?

5. **Q:** Are Christians to meet on the seventh day? **Q:** What was the practice and teaching of the early church? **Q:** Is it scriptural to call Sunday "the Christian Sabbath?"

6. **Q:** How should we use the Old Testament today? **Q:** What benefits does it have for us?

Assignment:

1. Complete the *Handbook* chart on Old and New Testaments.

2. Study the *Handbook* section about salvation.

LESSON 8
SALVATION

Plan for the Lesson:

1. Review the worksheet on the two covenants.
2. Look at each of the conversion stories listed below and answer the following question about each. **Q:** What specific things does the passage say the person or group did or was told to do to be saved?
    a.   Acts 2:36-38
    b.   Acts 8:12
    c.   Acts 8:34-38
    d.   Acts 9:5-9,18; 22:14-16
    e.   Acts 10:47-48
    f.   Acts 16:14-15
    g.   Acts 16:30-33
    h.   Acts 18:8

    Q: From this survey, what would you conclude was the teaching of the apostles about how a person was to come to Christ to be saved?
3. **Q:** Who is in need of forgiveness?
4. **Q:** From the Scriptures, how would you answer the following questions about baptism?
    a.   **Q:** What does the Bible teach one must do before being ready to be baptized?
    b.   **Q:** By what manner were people always baptized in the New Testament?
    c.   **Q:** What reasons does the New Testament give for people to be baptized?
5. Study the following chart and be able to explain it.

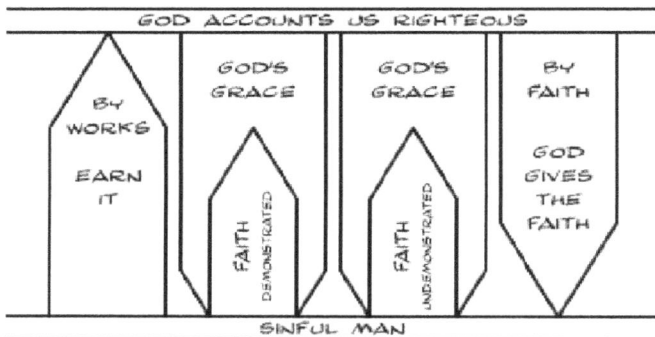

(Teacher: For an explanation of this chart, go to the chapter on Salvation by Faith in *How to Explain* or to the same lesson on www.oc.edu/faculty/stafford.north/pe.)

Assignment:
1. Complete the *Handbook* chart on salvation.

LESSON 9
SALVATION—Part 2

Plan for the Lesson:

1. Check the worksheet on salvation.

2. **Q:** How would you respond to someone who says, "Since Romans 5:1 says we are 'justified by faith,' one must be saved as soon as he/she believes in Jesus"?

3. **Q:** Discuss as many of the following statements as you have time for to see whether they properly express the view of Scripture about salvation.

   a. From Lenski's commentary on Acts 2:42 on the mode of baptism used on Pentecost. "One mode, however, was not used: immersion. The church [now] has selected the simplest mode, one that is probably much like the one that was employed in Jerusalem. . . . The most ancient tracings and carvings portray the act of baptism as being carried out by pouring. In this way, John baptized Jesus, and in this way other baptisms were administered." (Consider passages such as Matthew 3:16; Acts 8:38; Romans 6:4. The pictures of baptism with somone pouring out something are attempting to portray something besides how one is baptized. What do you think that might be?)

   b. NIV Study Bible, p. 1648, commenting on Acts 2:38. "Not that baptism effects forgiveness. Rather, forgiveness comes through that which is symbolized by baptism." On Romans 6:4. the NIV adds this. "In NT times baptism so closely followed conversion that the two were considered part of one event (see Ac 2:38 and note). So although baptism is not a means by which we enter into a vital faith relationship with Jesus Christ, it is closely associated with faith. Baptism depicts graphically what happens as a result of the Christian's union with Christ, which comes through faith—through faith we are united with Christ, just as through our natural birth we are united with Adam. As we fell into sin and became subject to death in father Adam, so we now have died and been raised again with Christ—which baptism symbolizes."

   c. From Lowell O. Erdahl in *10 Habits for Effective Ministry*, p 18. "To avoid preaching cheap grace, some proclaim *conditional grace*, which is not grace at all. It's only another form of work righteousness that turns us back toward more self-centered struggling and deeper dependence upon ourselves. . . . the gracious God we know in Christ does promise to save us without our help."

d. From A. T. Robertson, quoted in Lenski's commentary on Acts, page 910, commenting on the purpose of baptism in Acts 22:16. "But with 'picturesque language' R[obertson] means that 'here baptism pictures the change that had already taken place,' i.e., that is all baptism does."

e. NIV Study Bible, p. 1690 on Acts 22:16. "Baptism is the outward sign of an inward work of grace. The reality and the symbol are closely associated in the NT (see 2:38; Tit 3:5; I Pe 3:21). The outward rite, however, does not produce the inward grace (cf. Ro 2:28-29; Eph 2:8-9; Php 3:4-9)."

Assignment:

1. Read the section in the *Handbook* on the Church.

LESSON 10
THE CHURCH

Plan for the Lesson:
1. **Q:** How would you define the word "church" as used in Scripture?
2. **Q:** What are different words used in Scripture to describe the church?
   Q: What do we learn about the church from each of these terms?
3. Study the drawing below and then discuss what it suggests are the differences between the scriptural view of the church and the denominational view of the church.

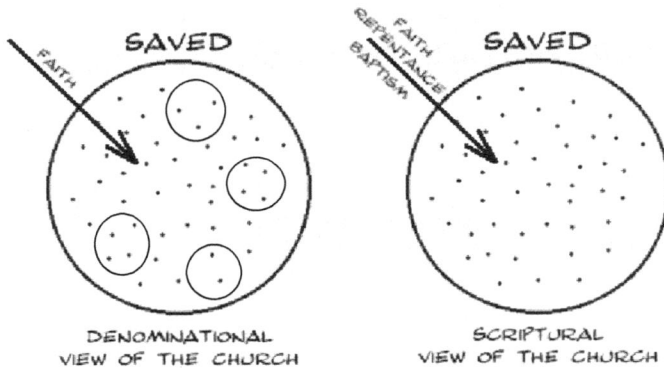

DENOMINATIONAL
VIEW OF THE CHURCH

SCRIPTURAL
VIEW OF THE CHURCH

(For more explanation on this chart see the chapter on denominations in the *How to Explain* Teacher's Manual or go to www.oc.edu/faculty/stafford.north/pe for the chapter on the Church and Denominations.)

4. **Q:** How would you respond to this question, "Do you believe only those in your church will go to heaven?"
5. **Q:** Is it possible today for one to be a member of the same church that the Christians in Jerusalem, Ephesus, and Rome were members of?
6. **Q:** If someone had asked a member of the church in Ephesus or Rome what church he/she was a member of, how might they have responded?

Assignment:
1. Complete the *Handbook* worksheet on Organization of the Church.
2. Assign different people to complete the *Handbook* chart on Worship for different churches.

LESSON 11
WORSHIP

Plan for the Lesson:

1. Review the chart on church organization.
2. Ask the persons assigned to report on their particular church as far as worship is concerned.
3. **Q:** What are ways in which different churches view the communion? **Q:** How would you state the scriptural view of the bread and the cup?
4. **Q:** How could individuals in this congregation likely improve their participation in worship?
5. **Q:** What are the figures of speech in the statement of Jesus that says, "This cup which is poured out for you is the new covenant in my blood" (Luke 22:20).

Assignment:

1. Complete the chart on worship for all churches.
2. Read the section in the *Handbook* on the topic of Last Things.

LESSON 12
LAST THINGS

Plan for the Lesson:

1. **Q:** Does Matthew 24:4-14 provide a list of signs by which people can tell when the end of the world is near?

2. **Q:** Does 1 Thessalonians 4:13-17 teach that there will come a time when living Christians will disappear while life goes on for everyone else? **Q:** In this passage, if dead Christians are raised "first," what event does the passage say will happen second?

3. **Q:** What is the most common description in Scripture to describe what Christ's second coming will be like? **Q:** What is this description intended to teach us? (See Matthew 24:43; Luke 12:39; 1 Thessalonians 5:2; 2 Peter 3:10.)

4. According to John 6:40, on what day will the righteous be raised? **Q:** What other things does the Bible say will happen on the last day? (See John 12:48; 2 Thessalonians 1:6-10.) **Q:** In view of these passages, how likely is it that life will continue on earth for 1007 years after Christians are raised?

5. **Q:** Does Revelation 20:4-6 teach that Jesus will return to earth to reign a thousand years?

6. **Q:** What does 1 John 2:18 and 22 teach about Anti-christs? **Q:** How many will there be? **Q:** When will they start coming? **Q:** What will they do? **Q:** How does this compare with the view often spoken about Anti-christs today?

Assignment:

1. Complete the *Handbook* worksheet on Last Things.
2. Do the worksheet on definitions. Leave blank any you do not know.

LESSON 13
ISLAM

Plan for the Lesson:

1. **Q:** How would you describe the current situation between Muslims and Christians?

2. **Q:** Do you believe the Muslims are more likely or less likely to be able to expand their religion to Western nations since 9/11?

3. Select some of the questions on Worksheet 13 about Islam and discuss them in class. If students have been assigned in advance to write their answers they can share them. If not, the class can work on the answers together.

4. **Q:** Does anyone in class have any direct contact with someone of the Muslim faith? **Q:** What have your experiences been? **Q:** How can we best reach out to such people?

Assignment:

1. Complete Worksheet 14 on Islam.
2. Prepare for the next lesson as assigned by the teacher.

LESSON 14
SUMMARY AND REVIEW

Plan for the Lesson:

1. Review the definitions and complete any not covered in the class.

2. Answer questions from the class.

3. Think of questions with which you might kindly begin a discussion with those of various religious beliefs.

4. If you have more time in other sessions, role-play discussions with those of different faiths.

Bibliography

A Discussion Between a Preacher and a Priest. Fort Worth: Leroy Brownlow Publications, 1953.

Adams, Hampton. *Why I Am A Disciple of Christ.* Toronto: Thomas Nelson & Sons, 1957.

Bales, James D. *The Book of Mormon?* Rosemead, California: Old Paths Book Club, 1958.

The Book of Mormon. Salt Lake City: The Church of Jesus Christ of Latter-day Saints, 1920.

Branson, William Henry. *Drama of the Ages.* Nashville: Southern Publishing Association, 1952.

Campbell, A. *Christianity Restored.* Rosemead, California: Old Paths Book Club, 1959.

Douty, Norman F. *Another Look at Seventh-day Adventism.* Grand Rapids: Baker Book House, 1962.

The Doctrine and Covenants of the Church of Jesus Christ of Latter-Day Saints. Salt Lake City: The Church of Jesus Christ of Latter-Day Saints, 1955.

Doctrine and Discipline of the Methodist Church 1960. Nashville: The Methodist Publishing House, 1960.

Dreyer, F.C.H. and Weller, E. *Roman Catholicism in the Light of Scripture.* Chicago: Moody Press, 1960.

From Paradise Lost to Paradise Regained. Brooklyn: Watchtower Bible and Tract Society, 1958.

Gerstman, John H. *The Theology of the Major Sects.* Grand Rapids: Baker Book House, 1975.

Gibbons, James Cardinal. *The Faith of Our Fathers, 83ʳᵈ Revised Edition.* New York: P.J. Kennedy & Sons, 1917.

Good News to Make You Happy. New York: Watchtower Bible and Tract Society and International Bible Students Association, 1976.

Gruss, Edmond C. *The Jehovah's Witness and Prophetic Speculation.* Nutley, NJ: Presbyterian and Reformed Publishing Company, 1974.

Hiscox, Edward T. *The Standard Manual for Baptist Churches.* Philadelphia: The American Baptist Publication Society, 1951.

Hoekema, Anthony A. *The Four Major Cults.* Grand Rapids: William B. Eerdman Publishing Company, 1963.

Hunter, Milton R. *The Gospel Through the Ages, Melchizedek Priesthood Course of Study.* Salt Lake City, 1945-46.

Kelcy, Raymond. *The Letters of Paul to the Thessalonians.* Austin: R.B. Sweet Company, Inc., 1968.

Kik, J. Marcellus. *The Eschatology of Victory.* The Presbyterian and Reformed Publishing Company, 1974.

Bibliography

Lanier, Roy H., Sr. *Mormon Doctrine*. Abilene, Texas: n.d.

Lanier, Roy. H., Sr. "A Study of Matthew 24," *Firm Foundation* (May 24, 31, June 7, 1977), XCIV, Nos. 21, 22, 23.

Let God Be True. Brooklyn: Watchtower Bible and Tract Society, Inc., & International Bible Students Association, 1946.

Life Everlasting—in Freedom of the Sons of God. Brooklyn: Watchtower Bible and Tract Society, 1966.

Manual of the Church of the Nazarene. Kansas City: Nazarene Publishing House, 1968.

Martin, Warter R. *The Kingdom of the Cults*. Minneapolis: Bethany Fellowship, Inc., Publishers, 1974.

McGarvey, J.W. and Pendleton, Philip Y. *Thessalonians, Corinthians, Galatians, and Romans*. Cincinnati: The Standard Publishing Company, 1916.

Mead, Frank J. *Handbook of Denominations in the United States*. New Sixth Edition. Nashville: Abingdon, 1951.

Miller, Park H. *Why I Am a Presbyterian*. Toronto: Thomas Nelson & Sons, 1956.

Odle, Joe T. *Church Member's Handbook*. Revised Edition. Nashville: Broadman Press, 1962.

The Pearl of Great Price. Salt Lake City: The Church of Jesus Christ of Latter-Day Saints, 1958.

Pendleton, J.J. *Baptist Church Manual*. Nashville: Broadman Press, 1966.

Riggs, Ralph M. *We Believe*. Springfield: Gospel Publishing House, 1954.

Roberts, J.W. *The Revelation to John (The Apocalypse)*. Austin: Sweet Publishing Company, 1974.

Rowe, John F. *The History of Apostasies*. Reevaluated and Augmented by John Allen Hudson. Rosemead, California: Old Paths Book Club, 1956.

Russell, Charles T. *Studies in the Scriptures*. 7 Vols. Brooklyn: Watchtower Bible and Tract Society, 1886=1917.

Russell, C.T. *Thy Kingdom Come*. Allegheny, Pennsylvania: Watchtower Bible and Tract Society, 1891.

Rutherford, J.F. *Millions Now Living Will Never Die*. Brooklyn: International Bible Students Association, 1920.

Selecman, Charles C. *The Methodist Primer*. Revised Edition. Nashville: Tidings, 1947.

Seventh-day Adventist Church Manual. General Conference of Seventh-day Adventists, 1959.

Seventh-day Adventists Answer Questions on Doctrine. An Explanation of Certain Major Aspects of Seventh-day Adventist Belief. Prepared by a Representative Group of Seventh-day Adventist Leaders, Bible Teachers, and Editors. Washington, D.C.: Review and Herald, 1957.

Shank, Robert. *Elect in the Son*. Springfield, Missouri: Westcott Publishers, 1970.

"Statement of Fundamental Truths," General Council of the Assemblies of God. Tract No. 34-4136. Springfield, Missouri: Gospel Publishing House, n.d.

Summers, Ray. *Worthy is the Lamb*. Nashville: Broadman Press, 1951.

The Truth That Leads to Eternal Life. Watchtower Bible and Tract Society, 1968.

Smith, George D. (ed). *The Teaching of the Catholic Church* Vols. I and II. New York: The MacMillan Company, 1964.

Talmage, James E. *The Articles of Faith*. 12th Ed. Salt Lake City: The Church of Jesus Christ of Latter Day Saints, 1924.

This Means Everlasting Life. Brooklyn: Watchtower Bible and Tract Society & International Bible Students Association, 1950.

Wallace, O.C.S. *What Baptists Believe*. Nashville: The Sunday School of Southern Baptist Convention, 1934.

You May Survive Armageddon in God's New World. Brooklyn: Watchtower Bible and Tract Society, 1955.

Young, Brigham. *The Journal of Discourses, 1901*.

www.ingramcontent.com/pod-product-compliance
Lightning Source LLC
Chambersburg PA
CBHW071433090426
42737CB00011B/1645